HISTORY

Curriculum Bank

KEY STAGE ONE
SCOTTISH LEVELS A-B

HISTORY

PENELOPE HARNETT

Published by Scholastic Ltd,
Villiers House,
Clarendon Avenue,
Leamington Spa,
Warwickshire CV32 5PR
Text © Penelope Harnett
© 1996 Scholastic Ltd
34567890   789012345

AUTHOR
PENELOPE HARNETT

EDITOR
JANE BISHOP

ASSISTANT EDITOR
SALLY GRAY

SERIES DESIGNER
LYNNE JOESBURY

DESIGNER
LOUISE BELCHER

ILLUSTRATIONS
MAGGIE DOWNER

COVER ILLUSTRATION
GAY STURROCK

INFORMATION TECHNOLOGY CONSULTANT
MARTIN BLOWS

SCOTTISH 5–14 LINKS
MARGARET SCOTT AND SUSAN GOW

Designed using Aldus Pagemaker
Printed in Great Britain by Bell and Bain Ltd, Glasgow

British Library Cataloguing-in-Publication Data
A catalogue record for this book is available from the
British Library.

ISBN 0-590-53396-7

Contents

Introduction

Scholastic Curriculum Bank is a series for all primary teachers, providing both an essential planning tool for devising comprehensive schemes of work as well as an easily accessible and varied bank of practical, classroom-tested activities with photocopiable resources.

Designed to help planning for an implementation of progression, differentiation and assessment, *Scholastic Curriculum Bank* offers a structured range of stimulating activities with clearly-stated learning objectives that reflect the programmes of study, and detailed lesson plans that allow busy teachers to put the ideas into practice with the minimum amount of preparation time. The photocopiable sheets that accompany many of the activities provide ways of integrating purposeful application of knowledge and skills, differentiation, assessment and record-keeping.

Opportunities for formative assessment are highlighted where appropriate within the activities, while separate summative assessment activities give guidelines for analysis and subsequent action. Ways of using information technology for different purposes and within different contexts, as a tool for communicating and handling information and as a method for investigating, are integrated into the activities where appropriate and more explicit guidance is provided at the end of the book.

The series covers all the primary curriculum subjects with separate books for Key Stages 1 and 2/Scottish Levels A–B and C–E. It can be used as a flexible resource with any scheme to fulfil National Curriculum and Scottish 5–14 requirements and to provide children with a variety of different learning experiences that will lead to effective acquisition of skills and knowledge.

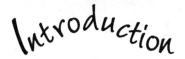

SCHOLASTIC CURRICULUM BANK HISTORY

This *Scholastic Curriculum Bank History* book is designed for teachers of Key Stage 1 History. It provides a range of activities which are closely linked to the requirements of the Key Stage 1 History National Curriculum. Many of the activities also cover areas in the Key Stage 2 History Programme of Study and Key Stage 2 teachers will also find them helpful for organising and planning work in their classrooms.

Aims of this book

Curriculum Bank History has been designed for teachers to plan, teach and assess history activities in the classroom. The lesson plans include background information and suggestions for developing children's historical skills and understandings. The lesson plans identify the Areas of Study and the Key Elements of the History Key Stage 1 Programme of Study. There are suggestions to help assess children's learning in relation to the History Attainment Target. Advice is provided on differentiation to take into account the children's abilities and stages of maturity at Key Stage 1.

The activities are planned to take into account the cross-curricular nature of the Key Stage 1 curriculum. Links with other subject areas are indicated and opportunities for developing history within popular Key Stage 1 topics are identified. The grid on pages 19–20 is designed to help plan historical activities within a topic approach. A icon in the lesson plans indicates where there are opportunities for developing work in IT.

Curriculum Bank History also provides guidance for planning a scheme of work at Key Stage 1. Criteria are suggested for the selection of historical content. Planning for progression is also addressed and advice is given on record-keeping and monitoring National Curriculum History.

Using this book

The book can be used in a variety of ways. Grids on pages 13–18 show how the activities can be used. The main chapter headings are linked to the Areas of Study in the Key Stage 1 Programme of Study. You can use the activities to provide an historical focus for thematic work in the classroom, for example the history of transport; houses and homes; food etc. Alternatively, the activities can be used to resource an in-depth study of an historical period eg; the Victorians; medieval times. Other activities relate to specific times of the year and anniversaries and can be used as appropriate. You can also 'dip into' the book and select particular activities most suitable for your own children. Activities which relate to the Key Stage 2 Programme of Study are also identified on a 'time' grid, which shows various periods of history and is found on pages 21–22.

Lesson plans

Detailed lesson plans are included for historical activities. They are designed to provide appropriate material for immediate implementation in the classroom. The structure for each lesson plan is as follows:

Activity title box

The information contained in the box at the beginning of each activity outlines the following key aspects:
▲ *Activity title and children's learning objective.* Each activity identifies learning intentions for the children. Reference is made to the Areas of Study and particular Key Elements in the Programme of Study for history.
▲ *Class organisation/Likely duration.* Icons ✝✝ and 🕐 indicate the number of children involved in the activity and the approximate duration of the activity. The book contains activities suitable for individual, paired, group and whole class work. Many activities involve whole class introductions prior to individual or group work. Some activities will continue and be extended over more than one lesson.

Previous skills/knowledge needed

Information is given here when it is necessary for the children to have experienced particular skills or acquired specific knowledge before undertaking the activity.

Key background information

This section provides information to extend teachers' historical knowledge and awareness about the activity. It is designed to set the activity within a broader historical framework and to elaborate on the context and skills addressed by the activity.

Preparation

Advice on preparation needed prior to the lesson is provided. Preparation of particular materials and reference to the photocopiable sheets is included as well as the organisation of a display or similar stimulus.

Resources needed

All the materials required for the activity are listed so that they can be assembled before the activity begins. Most lesson plans can be supplemented with additional books, pictures and posters to stimulate children's interest.

What to do

Clear instructions are provided for carrying out the tasks. Specific questions to ask the children are included and points to develop through discussion are identified.

Suggestion(s) for support/extension

Advice on how the activities might be adapted to meet children's different learning needs is included. Modifications for both the less able and the more able are included.

Assessment opportunities

Key questions are provided which can be used to help assess children's learning in history.

Opportunities for IT

The icon ⊕ indicates where the activity might be extended to include opportunities for children to include information technology in their work.

Display ideas

Diagrams and notes for display ideas are incorporated within the activity plans as appropriate.

Reference to photocopiable sheets.

Where photocopiable sheets accompany an activity a small reproduction is included in the lesson plan. Guidance notes for the use of the sheets are included and if appropriate, examples of children's possible responses are shown.

Cross curricular links

The History National Curriculum is closely linked with the English National Curriculum and provides many opportunities for developing children's speaking and listening, reading and writing abilities. Links with other curriculum areas are identified in the grid on page 160.

Photocopiable worksheets

Many of the activities are accompanied by photocopiable worksheets. These can be used to develop historical skills and concepts and to provide opportunities for children to record and communicate their historical knowledge and understanding. Some worksheets can also be used as historical sources to provide the children with historical information. Others provide material for craft/colouring/painting or modelling activities designed to stimulate children's interest in the past. Certain worksheets will be appropriate for assessment purposes and would be useful as records to include in portfolios of children's work to monitor their progression in historical understanding.

NATIONAL CURRICULUM HISTORY KEY STAGE 1

Programme of study

The focus statement underpins all the teaching at Key Stage 1 and should be used as the guide for planning and teaching. The historical content to be taught is outlined in the Areas of Study. The Key Elements describe ways of developing children's historical understanding.

Areas of Study

The Areas of Study in the history curriculum outline the historical knowledge and information which children should be taught at Key Stage 1. They are flexible and permit teachers to exercise a certain degree of choice in the activities which they teach.

Curriculum Bank History covers all the Key Stage 1 Areas of Study. The book is organised within the following chapter headings:

▲ Myself and my family.

▲ Ways of life in the past, which covers the areas of: clothes; diet; everyday objects; houses; shops and other buildings; jobs; transport; entertainment.

▲ Famous men and women.

▲ Past events, festivals and celebrations.

Key Elements

The Key Elements act as a guide for planning work in the Areas of Study. The Key Elements may not be present in all the Areas of Study but should be covered by the end of Key Stage 1, consequently schools will need to consider where they are going to be addressed in their curriculum plans and history schemes of work. For advice and points to consider in developing whole school plans see page 12.

There are five Key Elements:
1. Chronology
2. Range and depth of historical understanding
3. Interpretation of history
4. Historical enquiry
5. Organisation and communication.

Chronology

The ability to sequence events and place objects in order is important in the study of history. Language is central for children to communicate their understanding and to describe their sequences. Numerical skills are also important. Children at Key Stage 1 need varied experiences to practise and develop important language and numerical skills to describe the passage of time. Such experiences could include:

▲ encouraging children to retell stories in the correct sequence.

▲ placing objects or pictures in historical order. Beginning with the oldest and finishing with the most recent.

▲ providing opportunities for sequencing activities in other curriculum areas. Use these activities to enrich children's understanding of time vocabulary, for example science – life

cycles of plants and animals; geography – seasonal change and the changes in the weather; religious education – celebrations and festivals; cooking and baking activities; birthday celebrations.

▲ creating personal timelines for children to sequence their own experiences and changes which have occurred in their life times.

▲ discussing the daily and weekly routines in the classroom.

Progression in Key Element 1 can be noted by children's increasing ability to sequence events and objects in their correct order. Children will progress from simple sequences employing terms such as yesterday/today, now/then, past/present, long ago, to using more complex vocabulary linked with the passage of time, including reference to particular periods for example the Victorians, medieval times.

Range and depth of historical knowledge and understanding

The National Curriculum emphasises the importance of stories to provide narrative and accounts of what happened in the past. Stories can help develop children's awareness that the past is different from the present. Important historical concepts such as cause and effect, and change and continuity can be introduced through stories. Classroom experiences to develop the range and depth of children's historical knowledge and understanding would include:

▲ introducing vocabulary about the past and ideas about past ways of life through stories.

▲ presenting a wide range of stories from different historical periods and cultures to provide children with a broad historical background.

▲ choosing a range of types of stories including both eye-witness accounts and historical fiction to familiarise children with the range of historical narrative.

▲ discussing why things happened and why particular events occurred.

▲ providing opportunities to recognise similarities and differences between present and past ways of life. Why have some of the changes in our ways of life taken place?

▲ looking at the effects of such events and changes and encouraging the children to explain reasons for their observations.

Progression in Key Element 2 can be noted as children become able to recount more details and information about episodes and ways of life in the past. They begin to recognise reasons for events in the past and to identify the results of main events and changes.

Interpretations of history

Children can learn about the past from many different sources. Essentially this Key Element emphasises the importance of secondary sources of information. These sources are dependent to some degree on interpretation; how the past has been perceived by people living at a later date. Artists' drawings and illustrations in history books

provide examples of particular interpretations of history; how do artists know what to draw? Some parts may be based on historical evidence and some others will be dependent on the artists' imaginations.

Children viewing films or TV programmes are looking at the producers' versions of the past. Are these accurate interpretations of events? The contents of museum displays are influenced by the available artefacts and also by the views of the museum curators who arrange the display.

This Key Element provides opportunities for children to question how historical knowledge and information about the past is handed down. In the classroom this Key Element can be developed through:

▲ encouraging children to question how we know about the past. Discuss the different sources of information available and encourage children to begin to identify whether the source is primary or secondary (that is – an interpretation of an event/way of life documented at a later date).

▲ discussing the sort of information which can be learned from different sources of information. Draw attention to the fact that some sources might be more reliable than others.

Progression in Key Element 3 will involve children recognising the different ways in which they can gain information about the past. They will be able to talk about the sources which they have used and what they have found out.

Historical enquiry

This Key Element emphasises the importance of primary source material as evidence for ways of life in the past. Sources to use at Key Stage 1 include artefacts, pictures and photographs, adults talking about their own past, written sources, and buildings and sites. In the classroom:

▲ encourage children to raise questions and look for answers from a range of source material.

▲ organise collections of different objects for children to investigate and to handle. Such collections can include both original and replicas of objects. Place old objects beside their modern equivalent to enable children to draw comparisons.

For example a Victorian flat iron beside a modern electric iron. Organise visits to local museums to view their collections; see if they operate a loan service. Pictures of objects from books and posters are also useful. Collections of old postcards and photographs can provide information about the locality. Family photographs can provide information for children about their earlier life. Also:

▲ encourage children to talk to older people about what they can remember, for example what was it like going to school in the past? What sort of toys did the children's parents play with?

▲ organise visits to different buildings and sites. Look for clues about past ways of life on short walks in the locality.

▲ provide examples of written sources of information for example old maps of the locality, copies of the school log book. Older children enjoy trying to decipher old writing with help. Transcripts of some of the writing might be helpful for more able readers.

Progression in Key Element 4 can be noted as children identify the different sources they have used to find out about the past. Children progress from simple to more detailed observations of particular sources and develop skills to make generalisations and to draw conclusions about life in the past from different sources.

Organisation and communication

This Key Element emphasises the importance of providing different opportunities for children to communicate their understanding. In school:

▲ provide opportunities for children to talk and to share their historical understandings in class, group and paired discussions. Listen to their comments and ideas to develop your own awareness of their understanding.

▲ provide children with opportunities to record their understanding in a variety of ways; painting, drawing, modelling, collage, photography, using cassette recorders.
▲ organise resources in the classroom to encourage role-play activities to develop children's historical imagination.

Progression in Key Element 5 could be noted as children begin to make some decisions on the best way of presenting the historical information which they have learned.

The History Attainment Target

The History National Curriculum has one Attainment Target to assess children's progress in historical knowledge and understanding. The level descriptions provide a means of recording children's progress in history throughout Key Stage 1 and are linked closely with the requirements for teaching history listed in the Key Elements. Children's progress is recorded by the level which provides the best description of their attainment at the end of Key Stage 1.

Curriculum Bank History has identified clear learning objectives within each classroom activity, and assessment opportunities which relate closely to these learning objectives. The suggested questions in the activities can be used for both formative and summative assessment purposes.

Use the suggested assessment opportunities to acquire information about your children's current skills, knowledge and understandings. The information which you gain from such assessments can help you in planning further learning activities designed to ensure the children's progress in history. At the end of Key Stage 1 ensure that you have gained sufficient information about the children's progress to make a summative assessment of their attainment.

Activities in *Curriculum Bank History* suggest a range of learning objectives and teachers can identify and select those which they wish to use for assessment purposes. Draw up a simple grid and enter the learning objective across the top and the children's names down the side. You may like to devise your own coding system to grade your children's learning. For example a scale ranging from A to E, describing children's understanding from excellent, good, satisfactory, some to none. Leave plenty of space on your grid for any specific comments.

Not all activities will be used for summative assessment purposes. However, making a grid provides opportunities to keep an ongoing record of selected activities which will provide a useful source of information for determining the level which provides the best description of the children's attainment across Key Stage 1. Children will need to have acquired a range of historical knowledge for their attainment to be recorded on the higher level descriptions.

Ways of assessing history at Key Stage 1

Children's progress in history can be assessed in a variety of ways. Listening to children talking about the past and describing different features of the past is important. Providing opportunities for children to develop their own points of views and listening to the reasons behind their opinions is helpful for evaluating their current understanding. Watching, listening and joining in with children's play provides informal methods for considering children's awareness of the past. Work with timelines is a useful way of assessing children's concepts of the passage of time and their historical language. Modelling, painting and drawing activities can be helpful for noting children's skills in observation. Gather together evidence from a range of activities to help make judgements about individual children's attainment at the end of the key stage.

Developing historical activities

The following suggestions provide some further guidance and ideas for extending children's general historical experiences in the classroom.

Timelines

Timelines are helpful devices to introduce children to chronology and to help them to record the passage of time. They can be used in a variety of ways and across different subject areas. Introduce children to timelines through simple sorting activities, for example now/then; old/new; things I did before I came to school and things I can do now. Children can plot their own histories on personal timelines. Family timelines and generation paths provide means of recording the passage of longer periods of time.

Photographs of different events at school can provide a visual account of the passage of time during the school year. Create a school or classroom timeline as a reference point

HISTORY KS1

QUESTIONS TO CONSIDER USING ARTEFACTS OR PICTURES

Describe
▲ What can you see?
▲ What is happening?
▲ What is it made of ?
▲ What does it feel/smell like?
▲ How big is it?

Purpose and function
▲ Why was it made?
▲ What was it used for?

Evidence
▲ What does it tell us about life in the past?
▲ Similarities between now and then; then and other historical periods?
▲ Why has it survived?
▲ Is it unique?
▲ Is it complete?
▲ Why was it made?
▲ Is it authentic/a replica?
▲ Is it a reliable source of information?
▲ Were there many of them?
▲ What else would you like to know about it? (Relate to other sources of information, for example, oral testimony, documents, buildings and so on.)

Time
▲ How old is it?

for children's historical experiences; pictures, artefacts and labels can be attached to the line. Children can add to the line throughout the year as they acquire further historical information. *Curriculum Bank History* suggests a range of different ways of organising time lines. For example, the activities on pages 26, 32, 52, 61, 64 and 72.

Artefacts and pictures

These enable children to engage in historical enquiries at first hand. Encourage children to undertake close observation and to question and speculate on the information which such sources can provide of past ways of life. Magnifying glasses are helpful for historical detective work. Placing an acetate sheet, divided into sections, over detailed pictures can be helpful to concentrate children's observations on particular areas. The grid opposite provides ideas to encourage children's historical questioning skills. Provide opportunities for children to ask the questions and listen to the points which they want to find out. *Curriculum Bank History* suggests several activities to encourage children to look closely at pictures and artefacts and to use them as sources of information.

Children can complete similarity and difference charts to record their observations (Example 1 below). They could also review current information and decide what else they would like to know (Example 2).

Example 1

> ### Looking at a Victorian flat iron.
>
> Things which are the same
>
> Same shape
> Has a handle
> smooth bottom
>
> Things which are different
>
> new iron has a plug
> old iron very heavy

Example 2

> ### Looking at a picture of a Victorian school room.
>
> Things I have found out
>
> oil lamp for light
> coal stove for heating
> rows of children not tables
>
> Things I want to know
>
> Did children like school?
> Was it cold in the school room?
> Who lit the coal fire?

Using books in the classroom

Organise a range of books in the classroom to resource historical activities and learning in the classroom. Many fictional stories are set in the past and provide opportunities for children to learn about different ways of life and different values. Illustrations in picture books can also provide useful historical information for children. Stories about families, young children and babies can be used to heighten children's awareness of their own personal histories. Encourage children to re-tell stories and to sequence events in the correct order. Children can try to identify the important episodes and features of different stories and to explain why they occurred.

There are many excellent historical reference books and children can be encouraged to 'read' the pictures as well as the written text. Children can also extend their information retrieval skills, by using content pages and indices to find answers to their particular historical enquiries.

Telling stories

Many of the activities in *Curriculum Bank History* involve telling children stories. Storytelling provides wonderful opportunities to pass on information about past ways of life. The plot of the story can be elaborated with many historical details. Present children with specific historical problems and involve them in the search for different solutions as the story is being told. Objects which can be used as props can make the story more interesting and engage the children's interest. The main points of the story can be written on small pieces of card to remind the storyteller about what to include. Several story-telling activities have been included in *Curriculum Bank History*. For example re-telling the story of Guy Fawkes (page 80), or the story of Grace Darling on page 86.

Classroom play areas

Children can develop their historical understanding through many play activities. Consider how play areas in the classroom can be adapted to relate to historical topics and to provide different props and resources for the children to use. The children would also probably enjoy creating an historical play area themselves which would provide them with many opportunities for researching the sort of objects and materials which they would need. Role-play can provide opportunities for children to imagine and to experience more fully what life might have been like in the past. Ideas for incorporating play areas in the classroom have been incorporated into several *Curriculum Bank History* activities. For example in 'The Mayflower' on page 105.

Planning the history curriculum at Key Stage 1

Curriculum Bank History aims to aid planning and the identification of clear learning objectives. In planning the History National Curriculum, decisions will need to be made at the whole school and classroom levels.

At school level consideration will need to be given to:

School level

▲ the allocation of time to cover the Areas of Study in History.

▲ the links with other subject areas and themes being developed in the school.

▲ the selection of thematic historical activities or patch history relating to a particular period in time.

▲ the depth of historical topics: some topics might be in outline.

▲ the record of children's historical experiences across Key Stage 1.

Historical content

▲ the selection of content from the Areas of Study crossing the Key Stage for example personal and family histories, famous people and events to be studied.

▲ the sequence in which the Areas of Study are to be taught across Key Stage 1.

▲ the coverage of different Key Elements.

Children's learning

▲ the assessment and recording of children's progress in history.

▲ the progression of children's historical understanding from Key Stage 1 into Key Stage 2.

▲ differentiation to meet children's different needs and abilities.

Resources

▲ the resources available within the school and community.

Classroom level

Teachers will need to consider:

▲ the selection of activities which cover the content of the Areas of Study and provide opportunities for children to experience the Key Elements.

▲ the ways in which children's historical language and vocabulary can be extended.

▲ the selection of appropriate historical source materials.

▲ the ways in which children's work can be assessed and used for planning future historical activities.

▲ the records of children's progress and attainment in history.

Make a grid to help plan your children's coverage and progression in the Key Elements. Use the heading Areas of Study and enter your data under: **Chronology; Range and depth of historical knowledge and understanding; Interpretations of history; Historical Enquiry; Organisation and Communication.** Enlarge your grid and use it to write down the relevant activities in the columns.

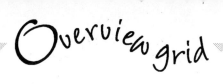

Learning objective	PoS/AO	Content	Type of activity	Page
Chapter 1: Myself and my family				
To develop an understanding of the passing of time in relation to changes in their own lives.	KE 1b, 4a. *Social subjects: People in the past: Change and continuity: Level B.*	Making a baby's catalogue.	Whole class discussion. Individual activity.	24
To recognise and describe changes in children's lives.	KE 1b. *As above: Level B.*	Children's awareness of changes in their lives. Sorting and grouping items.	Whole class discussion followed by group sorting activity.	25
To develop a sense of chronology by making a timeline sequencing personal events and changes.	KE 1a, 1b. *Time and historical sequence: Level B.*	Children's awareness of changes in their own lives. Drawing their own timeline.	Whole class discussion followed by individual drawings. Paired sequencing activity.	26
To gain an understanding of the concept of generation.	KE 1a, 1b. *As above.*	Children's awareness of generations in their family. Playing a generation game. Recording family generations.	Whole class activity, followed by individual.	27
To sequence familiar events and gain experience in using timelines.	KE 1a, 1b. *As above.*	Sorting photographs of different classroom activities morning/ afternoon.	Group and paired work for sorting and sequencing activities.	28
To acquire information from different sources and make comparisons with ways of life at different times.	KE 2c, 4a. *People, events and societies of significance in the past: Level B.*	Using different sources of information to find out about clothes in the past and comparing with those worn now. Recording.	Whole class discussion followed by pairs. Class review and individual recording.	29
To identify the ways in which the past can be interpreted by exploring museum displays.	KE 2c, 3a, 4a. *The meaning of heritage. Historical evidence: Level B.*	Sorting and grouping toys. Discussing museum representation of a Victorian nursery. Creating modern museum display.	Whole class discussion followed by individual or small group work.	30
To describe and sequence different homes using a timeline.	KE 1a, 1b, 2c. *Time and historical sequence: Level B.*	Modern homes,and comparing with those in the past. Homes timeline.	Class discussion followed by individual sequencing activity.	32
To develop experience of describing the passage of time.	KE 1a, 1b. *Time and historical sequence: Level A.*	Birthdays. Balloon display to record months children were born.	Class discussion. Individual drawing of self for balloon display.	33
Chapter 2: Ways of life in the past				
To learn about changes in sportswear.	KE 2c, 4a. *Change and continuity: Level B.*	Comparing modern and Victorian sportswear. Recording differences.	Whole class discussion followed by individual activity.	36
To find out about and sequence the process of woollen cloth- making.	KE 1a, 1b, 2b. *Historical evidence: Level B.*	Discussion on making woollen cloth. Sequencing the process.	Whole class discussion, followed by individual activity.	37

Learning objective	PoS/AO	Content	Type of activity	Page
To find out about the way of life in the past through a study of coats of arms.	KE 2b, 4a. *People, events and societies...* *Historical evidence: Level B.*	Discussion on coats of arms. Designing own coat of arms.	Class discussion. Individual designs of coats of arms.	39
To identify differences between ways of life at different times. To identify different ways in which the past is represented; songs.	KE 2c, 3a. *People, events and societies...: Level B.*	Storytelling a medieval banquet. Sing a Song of Sixpence. Drawing individual surprise pies.	Whole class storytelling, followed by individual recording.	40
To learn how flour was made in the past and to investigate how mills have developed over time.	KE 2b, 2c. *Change and continuity, cause and effect: Level B.*	Discussion on flour-making process. Constructing own flour mills.	Whole class introduction followed by individual/ paired model-making.	41
To use different sources of information to investigate ways in which children learned to write.	KE 2c, 4a. *Historical evidence: Level B.*	Different writing materials in the past. Making 'My writing book'.	Class discussion followed by individual bookmaking activity.	42
To identify differences between modern and Victorian laundry cycles. To draw conclusions from their findings.	KE 2b, 2c, 4a. *Change and continuity...;* *Historical evidence: Level B.*	Modern laundry cycle. Comparing Victorian artefacts.	Class discussion. Individual work completing photocopiable sheet.	44
To extend awareness of the importance of recording time. To investigate time-keeping devices from the past.	KE 2b, 2c, 4a. *As above: Level B.*	Discussion on ways of recording time. Making clock models.	Group sorting activity followed by paired work.	45
To compare different ways of lighting homes and describe the effect of lighting on people's lives.	KE 2b, 2c. **Technology: Design Process:** *Design and manufacturing processes: Level B.*	Sorting different lights and labelling.	Class discussion. Group, paired or individual model-making activity.	47
To compare modern water supplies with the past.	KE 2b, 2c. *Change and continuity... Level B.*	Discussion on the supply of water to homes, now and in the past.	Class discussion followed by individual work.	48
To compare a modern kitchen with a Victorian kitchen.	KE 2b, 2c, 4a. *As above: Level B.*	Recording data about modern kitchens and comparing with a Victorian kitchen. Modelling a Victorian kitchen.	Class discussion followed by paired discussion. Paired/individual model-making.	50
To describe and compare different kitchens. To organise a kitchen timeline.	KE 1a, 1b, 2c. *Time and historical sequence: Level B.*	Modern kitchens and ways of cooking. Looking at kitchens in the past. Kitchen timeline.	Class introduction followed by paired/ individual work.	52
To learn about the history of London Bridge and how it is remembered through rhymes.	KE 3a. *People, events and societies...: Level B.*	Play 'London Bridge is Falling Down'. Discussion on the origins of the song and the importance of London Bridge in the past.	Whole class activity and discussion.	53

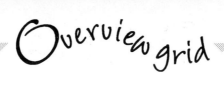

Learning objective	PoS/AO	Content	Type of activity	Page
To find out about aspects of the past from buildings and sites.	KE 2b. *Historical evidence* **Technology: Design Process:** *Design and manufacturing processes: Level B.*	Discussion on how castles were built and defended. Model-making castles.	Whole class discussion, followed by individual/ paired activity.	54
To identify different ways in which the past is represented. To use a range of information sources.	KE 3a, 4a. *Historical evidence: Level B.*	Sources of evidence about life in castle times. Drawing a reconstruction of a ruined castle.	Class discussion. Individual work.	55
To learn about the way goods were sold in the past.	KE 2b, 2c. *People, events and societies...: Level B.*	Singing street cries and rhymes. Design and make own street trader.	Class discussion and singing activity. Individual work making street trader.	56
To learn about shops and shopping in the past and to draw comparisons with today.	KE 2b, 2c. *Historical evidence: Level B.*	Investigating shops in the past. Designing shop signs.	Class discussion. Individual designs for shop signs.	58
To compare Victorian and modern classrooms and consider ways of representing the past.	KE 2c, 3a. *As above: Level B.*	Comparing a Victorian schoolroom with the children's own classroom. Artists' reconstructions.	Class discussion. Paired discussion using photocopiable sheet.	60
To examine bridges as sources of evidence about past life.	KE 2c, 4a. *Time and historical sequence: Level B.*	Function of bridges. Different bridge designs. Sorting and grouping bridges. Bridge timeline.	Class discussion. Group discussion. Paired sorting and grouping activity.	61
To learn about the harvest cycle and compare farming in the past with methods used today.	KE 2b, 2c. *Change and continuity...: Level B.*	Comparing modern farming methods with those in the past.	Class discussion. Individual recording.	63
To learn about the changing designs in fire-fighting equipment.	KE 1a, 2c. *Historical evidence; Time and historical sequence: Level B.*	Using pictures to describe fire-fighting in the past. Fire-fighting timeline.	Class discussion, followed by paired discussion. Class review. Paired or individual timelines.	64
To learn about motoring at the turn of the century from different sources.	KE 2c, 4a. *Historical evidence: Level B.*	Modern cars and motoring. Using photocopiable sheet as source of information about motoring in the past.	Class discussion. Individual labelling activity.	65
To compare modern bicycles with a Victorian penny farthing.	KE 2c. *Change and continuity...: Level B.*	Modern bikes. Measuring a penny farthing's wheels. Drawing a picture of a modern bicycle to emphasise differences.	Class and paired discussion. Individual recording of modern bicycle.	67
To use the Bayeux tapestry as a source of information about shipbuilding in the past.	KE 2a, 4a. *As above: Level B.*	Modern ships. Investigating and miming the shipbuilding process using the Bayeux tapestry as a source. Drawing the completed ship.	Class discussion. Group miming activity. Individual drawings.	68

Learning objective	PoS/AO	Content	Type of activity	Page
To consider the changes in transporting goods and how canals were used.	KE 2b, 2c. *As above: Level B.*	Discussion comparing transport of goods now and in the past. Importance of canals and how they worked. Completing picture.	Class discussion. Individual drawing to complete picture of a barge.	70
To learn about street vehicles 100 years ago and make comparisons with modern vehicles.	KE 2c. *As above: Level B.*	Acquiring information about street vehicles in the past. Comparing and drawing modern vehicles alongside vehicles in the past.	Discussion on modern and old vehicles. Individual drawing activity.	71
To sequence the developments in rail travel.	KE 1a, 1b. *Time and historical sequence: Level B.*	Similarities and differences between trains on the photocopiable sheet. Train timeline.	Class introduction, paired observations. Class review. Individual/paired sequencing activity.	72
To use evidence from a Victorian postcard scene to describe a Victorian holiday.	KE 2c, 4a. *Change and continuity...: Level B.*	Similarities and differences between now and Victorian times. Writing a Victorian postcard.	Class introduction and discussion of Victorian seaside life. Individual writing message.	74
To acquire information about Victorian holidays from looking at artefacts. To make comparisons with modern objects.	KE 2c, 4a. *As above: Level B.*	Similarities and differences between now and Victorian times. Items taken today.	Class discussion on contents of the Victorian suitcase. Individual drawings.	76
To examine the similarities and differences in playground games, past and present.	KE 2c, 4a. *As above: Level B.*	Photographs of modern playground games. Comparing with games from 100 years ago. Then and now pictures.	Class discussion. Individual drawings.	77
Chapter 3: Famous men and women				
To learn about Guy Fawkes and the Gunpowder Plot. To sequence the main events of the story chronologically.	KE 1a, 1b, 2a, 2b, 3a. *People, events and societies...: Level B.*	Guy Fawkes. Re-telling the story from Guy's point of view.	Whole class discussion. Individual story-writing.	80
To learn about the legend of King Arthur and how versions of stories can change over time.	KE 2a, 3a. *People, events and societies... Historical evidence: Level B.*	Chinese whispers. King Arthur. Creating different versions through role-play.	Whole class game and story. Small groups for role-play.	81
To learn about and sequence aspects of the life of Mary Seacole.	KE 1a, 1b, 2a. *As above: Level B.*	Sequencing pictures of Mary Seacole's life to make a book,	Whole class discussion and story. Paired/individual sequencing activity.	83
To learn about Dick Turpin and travel in the past.	KE 1a, 2a. *As above: Level B.*	Story of Dick Turpin – travelling in the past.	Group role-play. Individual poster-making.	84
To learn about the story of Grace Darling, considering different accounts. To discuss commemoration.	KE 2a, 2b. *As above: Level B.*	Modern life boat service. Grace Darling's rescue of survivors from a shipwreck. Designing a medal.	Whole class discussion and story. Individual medal designs.	86

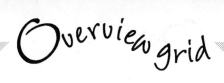

Learning objective	PoS/AO	Content	Type of activity	Page
To learn about Samuel Plimsoll and his load line.	KE 2a, 2b. *As above: Level B.*	Observing objects floating and sinking. Samuel Plimsoll. Testing Plimsoll load lines.	Paired/group activity at water tray. Class story. Paired activity marking Plimsoll line.	87
To find out about the life of Queen Elizabeth I and her portrayal in portraits.	KE 4a. *As above: Level B.*	Close observation of portraits of Elizabeth 1st. Painting own portraits of Elizabeth.	Paired observation and discussion. Class review. Individual painting.	88
To learn about St Hilda and ways of life in Anglo-Saxon England.	KE 2a, 4a. *As above: Level B.*	St Hilda, and her interest in collecting a library. Making books – illuminated letters.	Class discussion. Individual illuminated letters.	90
To learn about John McAdam's developments in road-building techniques, and how these affected people's way of life.	KE 2a, 2b. *Change and continuity... People, events and societies...* **Science: Earth and Space:** *Materials from earth: Level B.*	Roads and road surfaces. John McAdam's improvements. Children building their own roads and testing surfaces.	Class discussion and story-telling followed by paired roadmaking.	91
To learn about the inventor John Logie Baird and the effect of television on people's life-styles.	KE: 2a, 2b, 2c. *People in the past: People, events and societies...* **Technology: In Society:** *Technology as it affects lifestyles: Level B.*	Comparing life styles before television and describing changes. Advert design for a television.	Class discussion. Individual advertisement designs.	92
To learn about the achievements of the first Emperor of China.	KE 2a, 4a. *People, events and societies... Historical evidence: Level B.*	Achievements of the 1st Emperor. Sources of information. Modelling Chinese army.	Class discussion about China and information about the First Emperor. Individual models of soldiers.	94
To learn about Emily Pankhurst and the campaign for female suffrage.	KE 2a, 2b, 2c. *People, events and societies... Change and continuity...: Level B.*	Selected children participating in decision-making. Discussion on decision-making. Emily Pankhurst and campaign for female suffrage. Writing a speech for Mrs Pankhurst.	Selected children for class debate. Whole class – story of female suffrage movement. Individual speech writing.	96
Chapter 4: Past events and celebrations				
To develop understanding of seasonal changes and ways of describing the passage of time.	KE 1a, 1b. *Time and historical sequence: Level A.*	Pictures of different seasons to sequence and describe.	Class discussion. Paired drawing and sequencing activity. Class review timeline.	100
To explore cultural and historical variations in the recording of time.	KE 1a, 2a. *As above: Level A.*	Chinese New Year. Names of years and order. Pictures of the animals' race.	Class discussion and story, followed by individual pictures.	101

HISTORY KS1

Learning objective	PoS/AO	Content	Type of activity	Page
To find out about an event using a range of sources. To sequence scenes from the Bayeux tapestry.	KE 1a, 1b, 2a, 4a. *Time and historical sequence People, events and societies...: Level B.*	The monarchy. Battle of Hastings from Bayeux tapestry. Sequencing pictures.	Class discussion and story. Individual/paired sequencing activity.	103
To learn about the story of the Mayflower and harvest celebrations in the USA.	KE 2a, 2b. *As above: Level B.*	Pilgrim Fathers and settlement in America. Objects taken to America.	Class discussion and story. Individual identification of objects.	105
To learn about the Great Fire of London from different sources.	KE 2a, 3a, 4a. *Historical evidence: Level B.*	Singing 'London's Burning'. Great Fire of London – discussion of sources, including Samuel Pepys. Children's own diary account.	Whole class story and discussion. Individual diary accounts.	106
To learn about the first moon landing from different sources.	KE 2a, 2b, 3a, 4a. *As above: Level B.*	Sources of information about the first moon landing. Model-making.	Class discussion. Group, individual, paired models.	108
To learn about the Olympic Games – a past event from a different culture.	KE 2a, 2b, 4a. *As above: Level B.*	The Olympic Games now and in the past. Sources of information. Reconstructing a Greek pot.	Class discussion. Individual/paired activity reconstructing the pot.	110
To learn about the Eisteddfod and the Garsedd of the Bards – a commemorative event.	KE 2a, 2b. *People, events and societies...: Level B.*	Iolo Morganwg encouraging spread of Welsh language.	Class discussion. Individual accounts of Iolo Morganwg.	111
To learn about Diwali and celebrating religious festivals.	KE 2a. *Heritage: Level B.*	Diwali. Making divas and rangoli patterns.	Class discussion. Individual model-making	113

Entries given in italics relate to the Scottish 5–14 Guidelines on Environmental Studies (Social Subjects: Understanding people in the past).

Note: Key Elements 4b (To ask and answer questions about the past) and 5a (To communicate their awareness and understanding of history in a variety of ways) are present in most of the activities. Consequently specific reference has not been made to them in this overview grid.

Topic grid

	Buildings	Celebrations and special days	Clothes	Entertainment	Famous people	Food and cooking	Health and safety	Houses and homes	Jobs	Ourselves and our families	People who help us	Schools	Shops	Transport
Myself and my family														
Babies catalogues			✓	✓		✓				✓				
Changes in children's lives			✓	✓						✓				
Children's timeline		✓	✓	✓						✓				
Generations										✓				
School day										✓		✓		
Family clothes			✓							✓				
Children's toys				✓						✓				
Homes timeline								✓						
Birthdays		✓								✓				
Ways of life in the past														
Sportswear			✓	✓										
Cloth making			✓						✓					
Coat of arms			✓						✓					
Medieval banquet						✓								
Flour making						✓			✓					
Writing										✓		✓		
Washday								✓						
Time keeping								✓						
Lighting homes								✓						
Supplying water							✓	✓						
Victorian kitchen						✓		✓						
Kitchen timeline						✓	✓	✓						
London Bridge	✓													
Castle building	✓							✓						
Ruined castle	✓							✓						
Street cries									✓				✓	
Shops and shopping	✓								✓				✓	
Victorian classroom	✓									✓		✓		
Bridges	✓													✓
Harvest						✓	✓		✓					
Fire fighting			✓						✓		✓			✓
Motoring changes			✓	✓						✓				✓

HISTORY KS1

Topic grid

	Buildings	Celebrations and special days	Clothes	Entertainment	Famous people	Food and cooking	Health and safety	Houses and homes	Jobs	Ourselves and our families	People who help us	Schools	Shops	Transport
Bicycle				✓						✓				✓
Ship building									✓					✓
Canals									✓					✓
Street vehicles									✓					✓
Railway timeline														✓
Victorian postcard			✓	✓										
Victorian case			✓	✓										
Playground games				✓						✓		✓		
Famous men and women														
Guy Fawkes		✓												
King Arthur					✓									
Mary Seacole					✓				✓		✓			
Dick Turpin					✓									✓
Grace Darling			.		✓				✓		✓			✓
Samuel Plimsoll					✓		✓		✓		✓			✓
Queen Elizabeth 1st			✓		✓									
St Hilda					✓									
John McAdam					✓				✓					✓
John Logie Baird					✓			✓						
Emperor of China	✓				✓									
Emily Pankhurst					✓									
Past events & celebrations														
Seasons		✓												
Chinese calendar		✓		✓										
Battle of Hastings			✓		✓									
Mayflower		✓	✓		✓	✓								✓
Great Fire of London					✓									
First moon landing		✓			✓									✓
Olympic games		✓		✓										
Eisteddfod		✓		✓										
Diwali		✓		✓		✓								

Time grid

	Anglo Saxon / Viking	Medieval	Tudor	17th century	18th and early 19th century	Victorian	20th century	Other
Myself and my family								
Babies catalogues							✓	
Changes in children's lives							✓	
Children's timeline							✓	
Generations							✓	
School day							✓	
Family clothes							✓	
Children's toys						✓	✓	
Homes timeline	✓		✓			✓	✓	
Birthdays							✓	
Ways of life in the past								
Sportswear						✓	✓	
Cloth making		✓	✓	✓	✓			
Coat of arms		✓	✓					
Medieval banquet		✓						
Flour making		✓	✓	✓	✓			
Writing						✓	✓	
Washday						✓	✓	
Time keeping	✓	✓	✓	✓	✓	✓	✓	✓
Lighting homes		✓	✓	✓	✓	✓	✓	✓
Supplying water	✓	✓	✓	✓	✓	✓	✓	
Victorian kitchen						✓		
Kitchen timeline	✓		✓			✓		
London Bridge		✓						
Castle building		✓						
Ruined castle		✓						
Street cries		✓	✓	✓	✓	✓		
Shops and shopping		✓	✓	✓	✓			
Victorian classroom						✓	✓	
Bridges	✓	✓				✓	✓	
Harvest	✓	✓	✓	✓	✓			
Fire fighting						✓	✓	
Motoring changes						✓	✓	

Time grid

	Anglo Saxon / Viking	Medieval	Tudor	17th century	18th and early 19th century	Victorian	20th century	Other
Bicycle						✓	✓	
Ship building	✓							
Canals					✓			
Street vehicles						✓		
Railway timeline					✓	✓	✓	
Victorian postcard						✓		
Victorian case						✓		
Playground games						✓	✓	
Famous men and women								
Guy Fawkes				✓				
King Arthur	✓	✓						
Mary Seacole						✓		
Dick Turpin					✓			
Grace Darling					✓			
Samuel Plimsoll						✓		
Queen Elizabeth 1st			✓					
St Hilda	✓							
John McAdam					✓			
John Logie Baird							✓	
Emperor of China								✓
Emily Pankhurst						✓	✓	
Past events & celebrations								
Seasons								
Chinese calendar								
Battle of Hastings	✓							
Mayflower				✓				
Great Fire of London				✓				
First moon landing							✓	
Olympic games							✓	✓
Eisteddfod					✓			
Diwali								✓

Myself and my family

The activities in this section provide suggestions for developing children's awareness of their own personal histories and those of their families. Children can be encouraged to begin investigating their own past, what they were like as babies and how they have changed in their own lifetimes. Such activities introduce children to key ideas associated with the study of history such as change and continuity, cause and effect, chronology. Looking for similarities and differences focuses children's attention on what has changed and provides opportunities for children to try and explain why they think these changes have occurred. A sense of chronology develops from a broad range of different experiences. Within the suggested activities children will encounter sequencing activities, and will also have opportunities to extend their temporal language and vocabulary.

Talking about family histories may need sensitive handling taking into account the different personal backgrounds of the children within the class. Resourcing such a topic can be dependent on the amount of help and support received from children's families. Learning about their personal and family histories provides opportunities for children to acquire information from a wide range of historical sources, such as pictures and photographs, artefacts (baby clothes, toys and equipment), documents (birth certificates, newspaper announcements, cards), and oral accounts from family members.

A BABY'S CATALOGUE

How children have changed since they were babies –
the passage of time.

†† *Whole class; individual.*

🕐 *Whole class 15 minutes; individual variable.*

Previous skills/knowledge needed

This activity draws on children's knowledge of themselves as babies.

Key background information

This activity enables children to focus on how they have changed since they were babies, it will enable them to experience learning about the past from a range of information for example from artefacts, documents, pictures and adults talking about the past.

Preparation

Introduce your work on babies by encouraging the children to talk about when they were babies. Invite a parent with a young baby in to talk to the children about how the baby is cared for: feeding; bathing; dressing and to tell them about the sort of things which the baby likes to do. Children could bring in objects which they used when they were babies and items relating to their birth for example hospital tags, baby arrival cards or copies of birth certificates. Make small books which children can use for their baby catalogue.

Resources needed

A collection of baby clothes, equipment and toys. Baby equipment and clothes catalogues from different shops. Pictures and photographs of babies. Cards welcoming the birth of a new baby. Books for children to make their own baby catalogue. Pencils, colouring materials.

What to do

Introduction

Start by looking at a birth announcement card and talk about the excitement a new birth creates in the family. Encourage the children to contribute some of their own family stories relating to celebrations when they were born. Ask the children what sort of things they think a baby will need. Look at the different baby equipment and toys from your collection. Talk about how and why they are used. Together make a list of all the things which a baby needs. Can the children think of ways of grouping these things? For example clothing, feeding, toys, keeping clean and moving around.

Development

Look at the baby catalogues from different shops and explain to the children that they are going to make their own catalogue. Hand out the books for the children to make their catalogues. Children can draw different baby items on different pages. They might choose to give separate headings

to their pages for example clothes, feeding time etc. As the children are working, encourage them to remember their own experiences as babies to provide them with language opportunities to talk about the past.

Suggestion(s) for extension

Children can include some written descriptions and prices for some of the items. They might like to add a table of contents at the front of their book and they could number the pages of their catalogues.

Suggestion(s) for support

Help the children to label their different pictures. Some children might prefer to cut out pictures from baby magazines to add to their catalogue.

Assessment opportunities

Listen to how the children talk about the past. Can they use words and phrases such as 'then', 'now', 'before', 'after', 'when I was a baby' appropriately?

Opportunities for IT

Use a simple art or graphics package to design congratulations cards. Either design the cards in full, using the art package or use a selection of simple 'baby' clip art to make the cards. Print out the designs and stick them onto card. Alternatively use specialised software such as *Card Shop* for designing the card and adding their own message to it.

Children could also use a word processor to write their messages for the cards. Older or more able children might also use a word processor to design their own birth certificate, deciding what information needs to be included, what fonts to use and how to position the text on the screen.

Display ideas

Make a 'newborn baby' display. Include items of clothing, equipment and toys which the baby might need. Add other items for example copies of birth certificates, hospital labels, newspaper announcements. Children can design and make their own congratulations cards.

GROWING UP

To become more aware of changes in children's lives.

†† *Whole class then pairs.*

🕐 *Whole class 20 minutes; groups variable.*

Previous skills/knowledge needed
This activity will draw on children's knowledge of their earlier life.

Key background information
This activity can develop from the baby catalogue activity and requires the children to look more closely at changes in their own life.

Preparation

Extend the baby display to include items required by toddlers and pre-school children as well as pictures of children of this age. Prepare photocopiable page 116 for children to work in pairs.

Resources needed
Collection of baby, toddler and pre-school children's equipment and pictures. Pencils, colouring materials, photocopiable sheet on page 116. Sorting hoops, scissors, adhesive, large sheets of paper.

What to do

Introduction
Look at some of the pictures/items from the resource collection, and talk about some of the changes which have occurred to the children, for example learning to sit up; crawl and walk; moving from milk to more solid food and being able to feed oneself; learning to talk; changing from sleeping in a cot to a bed.

Development
Hand out the photocopiable sheet to pairs of children and talk about some of the items shown. Ask the children, working in pairs, to cut out the pictures and to think of different ways to sort and group them for example, items associated with eating; toys; moving around. Talk about the different ways they have chosen to sort and why they have put pictures in different groups. Ask the children to sort the pictures into items used 'before I came to school' and items used 'now I am at school'. Some items might overlap into both groups for example, books, teddy.

Conclusion
When you have discussed their groupings, the children can colour and stick the pictures onto a chart.

Suggestion(s) for extension
Children could draw some pictures of their own to add to the chart.

Suggestion(s) for support
Some children may need help with the sorting activities.

Assessment opportunities
Listen to children's use of vocabulary and phrases used to talk about the past. Note the different reasons they give for sorting and grouping the pictures. Can the children explain themselves clearly?

Opportunities for IT
Children could use a word processor to write labels for a class display, or to write comparisons between their lives before and after they came to school.

Display ideas
Display the children's charts under large headings, 'Before I came to school' and 'Now I am at school'. Write labels which invite the children to make comparisons between their lives before and after they came to school.

Reference to photocopiable sheet
The photocopiable sheet on page 116 shows pictures of a push chair, baby's feeding beaker, children's bicycle, bowl and spoon, plate of food with a knife and fork beside it, cot, bunk beds, bath, baby bath, books, rattle, teddy.

25

TIMELINE

To sequence events and changes in the children's lives and to use a timeline to record them.

†† *Whole class; individual; pairs; individual.*

○ *Whole class 10 minutes; individual 10 minutes; pairs 5 minutes; individual 15 minutes.*

Previous skills/knowledge needed

Children will need to have spent time talking about babies and changes that occurred in their earlier life. This activity will also draw on children's sequencing abilities.

Key background information

Timelines are a useful device for children to be able to record the passage of time pictorially.

Preparation

Ask the children to bring in a photograph of themselves when they were babies.

Resources needed

The children's baby photographs. Books and other pictures of babies and toddlers. Three pieces of paper about 10cm square for each child. Pencils, colouring materials, adhesive. A strip of card, about 10cm x 30cm for each child's timeline.

What to do

Introduction

Look at all the baby photographs. Can the children recognise each other when they were babies? Talk with the children about how they have changed. Consider size; things that they can do now – walking, speaking, eating on their own etc; clothes which they wear and toys which they play with.

Development

Hand out three pieces of paper to each child. Ask the children to draw themselves when they were babies on one piece of paper, when they were about three on the second piece and themselves now on the third. Tell the children to draw carefully, thinking about the size of themselves, what they looked like and what they were able and can remember doing. Ask them not to include any dates or numbers on the pictures.

Conclusion

When the pictures have been finished, ask the children to pass them on to a partner who should sequence them in the correct order, beginning with the youngest. Partners can explain what clues they looked for on the pictures which guided them in arranging the sequence. When they have been correctly ordered, children can stick their own pictures onto a strip of card to show their timeline.

Suggestion(s) for extension

The children can add more pictures to their sequence. For example 'when I was a tiny baby'; 'when I was one'; two etc. Children might also like to project into the future for example 'When I am twenty'.

Suggestion(s) for support

For some children limit the number of pictures to two if necessary, representing their babyhood and the present at school. These can be used for a 'then and now' timeline.

Assessment opportunities

Listen to how the children talk about the past and the vocabulary which they use. Can they recognise a sequence of changes in their own lives and explain them?

Opportunities for IT

Children could use simple graphing software to draw graphs about their birth weights. Working in groups the children can collect their birthweights and enter these into the software to provide simple block graphs.

Alternatively children could record their information in a database which could be set up in advance by the teacher. This would need to be kept simple for younger children and may only contain a small number of fieldnames:

name	John
sex	boy
birth weight	3kg
birth height	50cm
weight now	17kg
height now	110cm

Children could then sort the database information into numerical order to find the tallest at birth, then resort to find the tallest now and see if it is the same child. They could also explore the database information for example, to see if girls weighed more at birth than boys, or if the tallest babies were the heaviest.

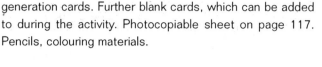

Display ideas

Display the individual timelines around a collection of photographs of the children when they were babies. Make a lift-the-flap display of each member of the class. Stick a photograph of the children when they were babies on a folded piece of card. Lift the flap to show a photograph or drawing of the children as they are now.

Find out the children's birth weights and lengths and make a comparison table. Using the birth measurements ask the children to draw a life size picture of themselves when they were born. Draw round the children now and cut out the figure so that they can make comparisons with themselves when they were babies. There are opportunities for IT here to collect, record and display data about children's sizes.

FAMILY GENERATIONS

To gain understanding of the concept of generation.
♦♦ *Whole class; individual.*
🕑 *Whole class variable; individual 20 minutes.*

Previous skills/knowledge needed

Children will need to have some knowledge of their own personal histories and that of their family members.

Key background information

Looking at different family generations provides children with opportunities to extend their experience of the passage of time within their own families and people close to them.

It will draw on children's knowledge of different members of their family and will need handling with sensitivity and awareness of the different personal circumstances of children in your class.

Preparation

Prepare cards with the names and pictures of members of different generations. For example brother; sister; mummy; daddy; aunt; uncle; nephew; niece; grandpa; granny; great aunt. Prepare photocopiable page 117, one for each child.

Resources needed

Pictures of different generations which could include pictures of different generations of the royal family. Prepared generation cards. Further blank cards, which can be added to during the activity. Photocopiable sheet on page 117. Pencils, colouring materials.

What to do

Introduction

Talk about the different generations within a family. Begin with talking about brothers and sisters. Then people who are the same generation as parents (aunts and uncles) and then grandparents. Look at the different cards with names of the members of different generations. Hand some cards out to individual children.

Development

Mark different areas off in the classroom/school hall/playground, and ask the children to start the generations. Children with cards of their own generation (brother, sister, cousin) can move into the first band. The second band would be for children's parents' generation, so children with mummy, daddy and aunt cards can move in here. Older friends of the family could also be included in this group. A third band could relate to their grandparents' generation. Once children have understood the different generations, this activity could be played as a game with children having to decide which band to stand in when a word is called out.

Conclusion

When children have some awareness of different generations, they can be asked to make their own generation path using the photocopiable sheet.

Suggestion(s) for extension

Some children may be able to go beyond their grandparents' generation to their great grandparents. Encourage children to research different generations within the royal family. They could be introduced to the diagram of a family tree.

Suggestion(s) for support

Children who find this activity difficult could focus on only their own and their parents' generation.

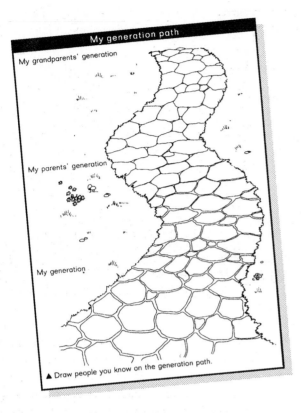

My generation path

My grandparents' generation

My parents' generation

My generation

▲ Draw people you know on the generation path.

Display ideas

Create a large display of pictures showing generations of the royal family or of some local notable family with appropriate titles. Children can draw and paint pictures of the different family members.

Reference to photocopiable sheet

The photocopiable sheet on page 117 shows a generation path which the children can complete.

TALKING ABOUT THE SCHOOL DAY

To provide opportunities for children to sequence familiar events, and experience in using timelines.
†† *Group then pairs.*
🕐 *Group 20 minutes; pairs 20 minutes.*

Previous skills/knowledge needed

This activity will draw on children's experience of events during the school day.

Key background information

The activity provides opportunities for children to gain experience of using timelines to record familiar situations.

Assessment opportunities

Can the children place family members in the correct generation? Listen to how the children explain where they have placed the family members. Have they appropriate language to describe the generations?

Opportunities for IT

Children could use a word processor to write the labels for a class generation chart. If this is of the royal family, for instance, they might add further information about each of the members on the chart. Load a format into the word processor such as:

Name
Date of Birth
Age now
Other information

Space could be left for children to fill in their own information or comments about a particular person.

Preparation

Take photographs of the children at different times during the school day. Stick the photographs onto durable card and laminate them if possible. Attach labels to show what is happening underneath the photograph. Hang a washing line with pegs across part of the classroom where the children can reach.

Resources needed

Photographs of the children. Washing line and pegs.

What to do

Show the children the pictures of the school day and talk about what is happening in the photographs. Group the children in pairs and ask them to sort the photographs into morning and afternoon activities. Can they sort the morning/afternoon activities further? For example before or after play. From these initial sorting activities ask the children to sequence the pictures to tell the story of the school day. Encourage the children to use time vocabulary for example, before/after; next; now/then to describe their sequence. Older children might refer to actual clock time. Peg the cards onto a washing line going across the classroom and encourage children to take the cards down and to reassemble them in the correct order of the school day.

Name:
Date of Birth:
Age now:
Other Information:

Suggestion(s) for extension

Children could draw other pictures and add them to the photographs to extend the sequence. The children could look at how the sequence might vary according to the particular day of the week.

Extend the activity by making a class timeline of important events occurring throughout the school year. Ask the children to try and put them in the correct order. At the end of the year, ask the children to select which photographs illustrate the most significant events during the year. Send these photographs up to the next class teacher so that the timeline will follow the children up the school.

Suggestion(s) for support

For a simpler task limit the number of photographs used to two, one showing a morning and one an afternoon activity.

Assessment opportunities

Are the children able to sequence the events correctly? Are they able to explain why they have arranged their sequence in a particular order? What sort of vocabulary and language are the children employing whenever they refer to the passage of time?

Display ideas

Use the washing line and pegs to create an interactive display where the children can be encouraged to sequence pictures of different activities occurring throughout the school day.

FAMILY CLOTHES

To find out about clothes worn by their parents and grandparents and to compare them with their own. To acquire information from different sources.

†† *Whole class; pairs; whole class; individuals.*

🕐 *Whole class 20 minutes; whole class introduction 5 minutes; pairs variable; whole class 15 minutes: individual 20 minutes.*

Previous skills/knowledge needed

Children will be expected to talk about the different items of clothing which they wear.

Key background information

Children are going to find out about clothes worn by different members of their family, using different historical sources, for example pictures, photographs, clothes and people talking about their own experiences.

Preparation

Encourage the children to ask their families for help in providing resources for this activity.

Resources needed

Collection of clothes and shoes belonging to earlier generations. Past photographs of members of the children's families. You might need to supplement these with a supply of your own! Old school photographs showing children at school in the past. Books, pictures and postcards of people showing aspects of their lives from the recent past. Pencils, crayons/felt-tipped pens.

What to do
Introduction

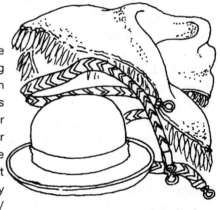

Familiarise the children with talking about their own clothes and clothes worn by other members of their family. Ask the children what sort of clothes they think their parents/ grandparents wore in the past? Compile a list of questions with the children which they can ask their families such as: What sort of clothes did they wear? What materials were they made of? Which were their favourite clothes? Did they have clothes for different occasions? Ask children to bring in old photographs of members of their families. They might also bring in actual articles of clothing and shoes.

Development

Review what the children have found out about the clothes worn by their parents and older relatives in the past. Introduce the idea that different sources of information can be used to find answers to their questions, for example photographs, pictures, clothes. Organise the children into pairs and hand out pictures, photographs and articles of clothing. Ask the children to describe their source of information. What

information does it give about clothes in the past? Ask the children to compare their modern clothes with their information. As children finish talking about one source of information ask them to return it to a central pool and to take another source of information to investigate. When children have investigated several sources, gather them together to pool their ideas and what they have found out.

Conclusion
Ask the children to record their observations in written and picture form.

Suggestion(s) for extension
Some children can add appropriate labels to their pictures to draw attention to the differences and similarities which they have noticed. Children might like to investigate clothes worn by generations in the more distant past.

Suggestion(s) for support
Some children might need help describing some of the features in the different sources of information. In this case the activity may be done together as a whole class and children's observations and pictures can be used to create a large classroom display.

Assessment opportunities
Listen to the sort of questions which the children raise – are they able to find the answers by looking at the different sources of information?

Opportunities for IT
Children could use a word processor to write labels for a class display of some of the clothes brought in. Show them how to change the font or make the text larger so that it can be read from a distance. Introduce bold text, underlining or centring. A simple desktop publishing package might also allow a border to be put around the label.

Display ideas
Display the different garments, pictures and photographs. Attach labels which encourage children to look for similarities and differences in clothing.

CHILDREN'S TOYS

To develop an awareness about how the past is interpreted by looking at Victorian toys in a museum and designing their own display.

†† *Whole class introduction; groups/individuals.*

🕐 *Whole class 10 minutes; groups/individuals variable.*

Previous skills/knowledge needed
Some awareness of museums and the objects which can be found in them would be helpful.

Key background information
The toys illustrated on the photocopiable sheet would be for middle class and rich Victorian children. Many toys at this time were made from wood and tin, although lead was used for toy soldiers and some animals. Clockwork toys were popular. Poorer children would make do with cruder, home made varieties, for example dolls made from wooden balls, stuck onto another piece of wood, with sticks for arms and legs; wooden soldiers roughly carved, with scarlet tunics and white trousers. Many games played in Victorian times are still popular today for example marbles, skipping, hoops.

Preparation
Prepare the photocopiable sheet on page 118, one for each child. Make a collection of modern toys. Use school toys and ask children to bring in some more from home.

Resources
Toy catalogues. Scissors, paper, adhesive, pencils, crayons/felt-tipped pens. Plain paper. Photocopiable page 118.

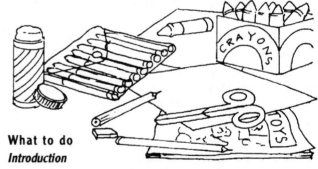

What to do
Introduction
Encourage children to find different ways to sort and group the toys from your resource collection, for example by size; age of children who would enjoy playing with them; materials; old and new toys and so on. Look for signs of wear on the toys. Are new toys always shiny? Do old toys always show signs of wear?
Development
Tell the children they are going to learn about toys which children played with a hundred years ago. Ask the children if they know of any toys which children might have played with then. Would they have played with the same toys as children do today? Hand out the photocopiable sheet and ask the

children to identify the toys on it. Discuss what the toys are made of and how they would have worked. Look for similarities and differences between the toys on the sheet and the collection of modern toys.

Conclusion

Explain to the children that the picture on the photocopiable sheet shows how a museum has arranged a collection of toys to give the impression of what a nursery, belonging to a wealthy family might have looked like about a hundred years ago. Ask the children to imagine they are going to create a museum display showing a modern children's room. What toys would they choose for their display? Would their display give an accurate representation of life now? Ask the children to draw pictures, or cut out pictures from catalogues of toys and arrange them to create a child's room of today. If their room was in a museum what things would the children need to explain to the visitors?

Suggestion(s) for extension

Children can talk about the objects which they have placed in their room for example: what they look like; how they are played with and what they are made with. They could write a museum guide to the room which they have created.

Suggestion(s) for support

Children needing some support can create a collage showing toys which would be found in a modern children's room. Children can draw their own toys and suggest information to go on different labels. Use the collage to draw the children's attention to similarities and differences between toys now and the toys on the photocopiable sheet.

Assessment opportunities

Can the children recognise any difficulties which museums might encounter in organising their displays? Can the children explain their choice of toys for the rooms which they have created? Can children suggest what people in the future might think of the room displays which they have created?

Opportunities for IT

Children could use a word processor, or a simple desktop publishing package to write labels for a toy display or to write the guide for their own display. Groups of children could write a guide highlighting just a few of the items in the class display. The tasks could be shared around the group with each child in the group selecting and writing about one toy. Prepare a format for the guide in advance with each child given an allotted space for their writing. An interesting design is a 'threefold' which takes an A4 sheet and divides it into three columns, or six if both sides are counted. If one column is left for a title, each child in the group can have one column for their writing including a space for an illustration which can be added

by hand later, or, if the school has a scanner added electronically on the word processed page. If children have access to a colour printer they can also experiment with colour to make their guide more attractive.

Display ideas

Use the collection of different toys for children to develop their own displays. Encourage the children to make their own labels and to explain why they have organised their display in a particular way. Children can often find different ways of displaying the same collection. Discuss the effectiveness of the different ways with the children. Use the display to encourage speaking and listening skills; ask a child to describe one of the toys carefully and invite the other children to guess which toy has been described.

Reference to photocopiable sheet

Photocopiable page 118 shows a reconstruction of a Victorian nursery in a museum. Visitors are looking at the toys which are in a roped-off section. The nursery resembles one which would have belonged to a wealthy Victorian family and includes: a rocking horse; a doll with a china face; a clock-work train; a group of lead soldiers; a dolls' house; wooden blocks with letters painted on them; a wooden ark with wooden animals; a theatre made from card.

Children's nursery - museum display

A HOMES TIMELINE

To describe different homes in the past and to sequence them in chronological order using a timeline.

†† *Whole class then individuals.*

🕐 *20 minutes whole class; 30 minutes individuals.*

Previous skills/knowledge needed

This activity requires children to be able to talk about and to describe their own homes.

Key background information

Photocopiable sheet page 119 provides examples of different homes from the past. The cave is the earliest type of home, providing very basic shelter.

The Viking home was built around a frame of wooden posts with wattle and daub filling in the spaces. The wattle comprised thin strips of woven hazelwood which was then plastered with daub; a mixture of earth, lime, cow dung, chopped straw and water. Sedge and reeds were used for thatching the roof. Inside, the floor was made of beaten earth. There were no upstairs rooms and the house comprised just one large room where the family would eat, sleep, work and entertain each other. There were no windows, except perhaps for a south-facing one so the room would be very dark and smoky.

The Tudor farmhouse was also built around a timber frame (generally oak since the wood is very strong and does not rot easily). The spaces between the frame were filled in with materials such as brick or wattle and daub. Most windows did not have any glass as this was expensive. Cooking took place over an open fire in a huge fireplace which provided heat for much of the house. The floors would have been made of brick, stone flags or timber. There were bedrooms and storerooms upstairs.

The Victorian terraced house was built from brick with a tiled roof. There were both upstairs and downstairs rooms, but still no bathroom. Cheap glass was used for the windows. There were fireplaces in all the rooms and a coal range in the kitchen for cooking.

The modern house is detached, and it has both a front and back garden and a driveway. There are large rectangular windows. Central heating radiators have replaced the coal fires (so there is no chimney) and cooking is undertaken using a variety of appliances in the kitchen.

Preparation

Ask children to look carefully at their own homes and be ready to describe them. This may need sensitive handling with some children. Take the children on a walk around the neighbourhood to help familiarise them with different buildings. Prepare enough of photocopiable sheet page 119 for each child. Make zigzag strips of paper or card for children to stick their house timeline on.

Resources needed

A collection of photographs of different types of houses within the school neighbourhood, pictures and books showing contemporary homes and houses in the past; various writing and colouring materials, photocopiable sheet (page 119), card or thick paper folded into a zigzag with six sections, scissors and adhesive.

What to do

Introduction

Talk with the children about their own homes – why are they important? Develop ideas such as warmth; comfort; shelter; food; leisure; sleep and so on. How can homes be described? Introduce different types – flat; terraced, semi-detached and detached houses; bungalow; mobile home; caravan. Materials used in construction – brick, stone, concrete, slate and tiles. Size – how many rooms? How many floors? Shape – of the buildings, windows, doors, roof.

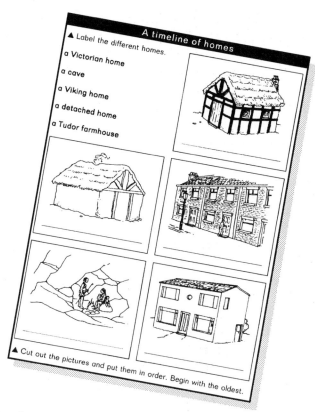

A timeline of homes

▲ Label the different homes.

a Victorian home

a cave

a Viking home

a detached home

a Tudor farmhouse

▲ Cut out the pictures and put them in order. Begin with the oldest.

Development
Discuss together the pictures of the homes on the photocopiable sheet, drawing on the earlier discussion.

Conclusion
Ask the children to cut out the pictures of the different homes and to arrange them in a sequence beginning with the oldest. Glue the pictures to the strip of card and fold the card into a zigzag to display the pictures. On the sixth space of the zigzag ask the children to draw a picture of their own home to conclude the sequence.

Suggestion(s) for extension
On the back of the zigzag card some children could write a description of the different homes. Research another building from the past or design a house for the future. Establish an estate agency in the classroom and encourage children to research details of different homes in the past which they can 'sell' to prospective clients.

Suggestion(s) for support
If necessary reduce the number of homes for children to sequence. Alternatively, ask the children to sort the homes into groups of 'now and then' and to try and give reasons for their choices.

Assessment opportunities
Can the children sequence the homes in the correct order? Listen carefully to their reasons; some children might live in similar types of homes as those depicted on the photocopiable sheet. Can the children describe the different homes and suggest what it would have been like to live in them?

Opportunities for IT
Children could set up a simple database about their homes. Each child could collect a range of information about their own home such as:

Name	Rachel
Address	Walker Road
Type	detached
Bedrooms	3
Garden	large
Garage	yes
Location	town

The fieldnames can be decided in advance or discussed with the class before the database is created. Once this has been done children can collect the data about their own house and then enter it into the class database. This might be done in pairs, with one reading and one entering the information. Younger children might need the support of another adult for this task.

Once the data has been entered children can use the database to answer questions such as:

How many children live in terraced houses? How many children have a large garden? Which is the most common number of bedrooms?

Some of the answers can be represented graphically using bar or pie charts, for example the most common garden size.

Display ideas
The zigzag books can be displayed alongside models of the different homes.

Reference to photocopiable sheet
The photocopiable sheet on page 119 shows pictures of a cave, a Viking home, a Tudor farmhouse, a Victorian terraced house and a modern house.

🖥 BIRTHDAYS

To develop children's experience of the passage of time.
To practise using common words and phrases relating to the passage of time.

†† *Whole class; individual work; whole class.*

🕐 *10 minutes whole class, 20 minutes individual, 15 minutes whole class.*

Previous skills/knowledge needed
This activity will draw on children's knowledge of birthdays and their own date of birth.

Key background information
This activity could be adapted in other ways to provide children with opportunities to talk about the passage of the months. Talking about birthdays might require sensitive handling with some children.

their drawing. Suggest they draw both a front and back view as the balloons are being hung from the ceiling. Cut out the drawings and place each one in the correct balloon basket. Display the balloons in the correct month order.

Use the balloon display as a discussion point to introduce children to vocabulary associated with time. Particular vocabulary and phrases to include would be *next/last month; before/after; now/then; first, second* and so on. Children will also become familiar with the names and order of the months. Keep the display up and use it as a point of reference throughout the year.

Suggestion(s) for extension

There are opportunities for using IT by collecting the data on children's birthdays on a data base. Discuss with the children ways in which the data might be displayed.

Suggestion(s) for support

Some children might need help with cutting out their pictures and writing labels.

Assessment opportunities

Are the children familiar with the months of the year? Can they sequence them in the correct order? Listen to the vocabulary and phrases which children use as they refer to the hot air balloon display.

Opportunities for IT

Children could use simple graphing software to display the data they collect about their birthdays as a bar chart. They could work in pairs or small groups to survey all of the children in their own, or other classes and then compare the graphs created. Younger children could use similar software which displays the information as a pictograph.

If the information was stored in a simple database children could extend their investigation by looking for patterns in the data. The fieldnames for such a database might be:

Name	Greg
Sex	boy
Month	June
Date	14
Year	1991
Day	Saturday

Now make a simple search to answer such questions as:

How many boys were born in May? What is the most popular day of the week?

Children could use the graphical facilities to plot graphs of birthdays in each month, or days of the week. The database could be extended to include other classes as well.

Display ideas

The hot air balloons can be attached to the wall or hung from the ceiling.

Preparation

Obtain a class list with children's dates of birth. In advance make twelve 'hot air balloons'. Cut out the balloon shapes from card and decorate them using collage materials. Beneath the balloon attach small baskets for the passengers. These can be cut out of card and painted or alternatively made from paper strips woven in and out. Label the baskets one for each month of the year. Hang the baskets beneath the hot air balloons using wool or string.

Resources needed

Pencils and crayons, thin card, adhesive, scissors, name labels.

What to do

Talk about birthdays with the children. Why are they important? What do they celebrate? How do children celebrate their birthdays? Ask the children if they know their birth dates; some children might need to be reminded. Discuss which children have birthdays in the same month.

Show the children the different hot air balloons and ask which balloon they would travel in to match their birthday, you could for example hold up the January balloon and ask which children would travel in that balloon. Ask the children to draw a picture of themselves and to attach a label with their name to

Ways of life in the past

The activities within this section provide opportunities for children to learn about everyday life in the past. Information has been included over a range of periods of time. Particular topics covered include: **clothes**, **diet**, **everyday objects**, **houses**, **shops and other buildings**, **jobs**, **transport**, and **entertainment**. Children's current understandings of familiar topics are used as a base for developing and extending understanding about life in the past for many of the activities. Children are encouraged to compare and contrast different ways of life suggesting reasons for differences which they have noted. There are opportunities for developing children's sense of chronology and sequencing abilities. Suggestions are made for helping children to acquire appropriate language and vocabulary to communicate the passage of time. The activities involve children in interpreting and acquiring information from a range of different historical sources.

Children are introduced to primary sources of evidence for example artefacts, pictures and photographs, adults talking about their own past, buildings and sites. They are encouraged to reflect on how the past has been interpreted through a variety of sources such as artist's reconstructions and illustrations, songs and museum displays as well as developing their own interpretations. Questions are suggested to help children develop their historical enquiry skills. The activities provide opportunities for children to communicate their understanding in different ways and include written accounts, drawings, paintings, model making and role-play activities.

VICTORIAN SPORTSWEAR

To learn about different sportswear worn in the past and to compare with sports clothes which are worn today.

†† *Whole class and individual.*

🕐 *20 minutes whole class; 20 minutes individual.*

Previous skills/knowledge needed
Children need to be able to talk about different clothes and their purposes.

Key background information
Football clubs grew in popularity from the 1860s onwards. The FA Cup was introduced in 1871. Well-dressed Victorian players wore long knickerbockers tied at the knee, long stockings, striped shirts, caps and ordinary leather boots with bars of leather nailed across the soles.

Tennis became a popular game, particularly for women, from the 1880s. No special clothes were worn and women must have found wearing their ordinary clothing very constricting and hot.

Victorian swimsuits covered a large part of the body. Knitted swimwear was worn, which stretched and became very heavy when it was wet. Cotton stockinette was another popular material for swimwear. Generally dark colours were favoured since the materials did not become transparent when wet.

Cycling became popular towards the end of the nineteenth century, after the introduction of the safety cycle, from 1885 onwards. Women wore knee length knickerbockers with long-sleeved blouses, tailored jackets and straw hats/boaters.

Preparation
Ask the children to bring in items of sportswear belonging to different members of their family. Prepare photocopiable sheet on page 120 enough for each child.

Resources needed
Catalogues and pictures of modern sportswear. Articles of sportswear worn today. Photocopiable sheet (page 120). Pencils, crayons and felt-tipped pens.

What to do
Introduction
Use pictures and examples of modern sportswear to talk about the special clothes worn for different sports today. Why do people wear special clothes? Talk about the different types of fabrics and styles used. Make a list of properties of good sportswear today. This might include durability; freedom of movement; colour and coolness.

Development
Explain to the children that they are going to look at sportswear which was worn in the past. Hand out the photocopiable sheet. Identify which sports the people are involved in, then ask the children to describe the clothes on the sheet and to compare them with their modern equivalents. Encourage the children to think of reasons for the older styles and what it would have felt like to wear them.

Conclusion
Ask the children to draw the modern equivalent of the clothes on the photocopiable sheet.

Suggestion(s) for extension ,
Children can write about the differences in the clothes which they have drawn. They might also like to research other clothes which were worn for different sports in the past.

Suggestion(s) for support
Some children may find the spaces too small on the photocopiable sheet for their drawings. Provide them with larger pieces of paper and use the photocopiable sheet as a source of information about sportswear in the past.

Assessment opportunities
Can the children identify differences in the styles of sportswear? Can the children describe what it would have been like to wear some of the clothes shown on the photocopiable sheet?

Opportunities for IT
Children could work in groups and use a word processor to make a class book about the way clothes have changed. Set up a format in advance and let the children write a short description of the changes.

Encourage the children with experimenting where they position their text on the page to leave room for pictures and

Victorian sportswear
▲ Draw what you would wear to do these sports today.

sportswear in the past. Draw pictures of people playing sports in the past. Add labels to draw the children's attention to how the garments have changed.

Reference to photocopiable sheet
The photocopiable sheet on page 120 shows a footballer; tennis players; male and female bathers; male and female cyclists dressed in the style of the late nineteenth century.

MAKING WOOLLEN CLOTH

To find out about the history of woollen cloth making.
To sequence the process of woollen cloth making.
†† *Whole class; individual.*
🕐 *Whole class 20 minutes; individual 30 minutes.*

Previous skills/knowledge needed
Some awareness of different fabrics which are used to make clothes would be helpful.

Background information
The art of spinning and weaving wool goes back thousands of years. Between 9,000 and 7,000 BC people began to herd sheep in flocks and to cut their fleeces using sharp flints. Wool from the fleeces was spun into yarn and used either for knitting or weaving into cloth. There is evidence from pictures on Ancient Greek vases which show women spinning and weaving. These were tasks which occupied members of the household for long periods. To make woollen cloth, first the wool was washed and then 'carded' that is, combed so that the thread all ran the same way. Special brushes with hard bristles were used for this purpose. The wool was then spun into yarn. Originally spindles were used for this. These had a heavy weight made out of clay, bone or stone attached to them. The wool twisted around the spindle as the weight was dropped. Later spinning wheels were used. The yarn was woven into fabric on a loom. Plants and vegetables were used for dyeing the cloth. Originally spinning and weaving were domestic and cottage industries, but following the invention of machines in the late eighteenth and early nineteenth centuries the cloth making process moved into factories.

The wool trade had been important in medieval England. Wool from British sheep was exported abroad and many merchants became wealthy through this trade.

to make their pages interesting. The pictures could either be drawn by hand or cut out from catalogues and stuck onto the page when it is printed out. Introduce the idea of saving the book at each stage and then retrieving the writing at a later date for printing.

If you have access to a scanner the pictures drawn by the children could be scanned and included on the word processed page. Children might also find other pictures from clip art collections or CD-ROMS.

Display ideas
Make a collection of modern sportswear to display. Ask children to use books and pictures to find out about

Preparation
Find out if there are any local groups interested in spinning and weaving who might have a member who could come in to school to speak to the children or who could lend any artefacts to you. Prepare a copy of the photocopiable sheet on page 121 for each child.

Timothy's football strip

Footballers used to wear long shorts

Look at some of our swimming costumes

Would you have liked to wear costumes like these?

Resources needed

Raw wool (washed), pictures of drop spindles and spinning wheels and looms, magnifying glasses, paper/card, scissors, adhesive, pencils, colouring materials, photocopiable sheet on page 121.

What to do

Talk about the raw wool. Which animals does wool come from? What does it look like? Pass some around. What does it feel like? Try looking at the different strands using a magnifying glass. Try twisting different strands between your fingers to make a thread.

Use the background information to describe the cloth making process and refer to any pictures from the resources. Hand out the photocopiable sheet and encourage the children to talk about what is happening in the different pictures. Ask the children to cut out the pictures and arrange them in the correct order to show the clothmaking process. After you have checked the order is correct and the children have explained the cloth-making process, the pictures can be glued onto a piece of paper in order. Develop this work by making some drop spindles so that children can try spinning their own thread. Children could try making some of their own weights from clay. Make some card looms for the children to try weaving their own woollen cloth.

Suggestion(s) for extension

Children can use the photocopiable sheet to make their own book about making cloth. Ask them to write underneath each picture what is happening in the scene. Look for pictures in other books which show people spinning and weaving in the

past. Children could experiment making their own plant and vegetable dyes for cloth.

Suggestion(s) for support

If necessary you could limit the activity to talking about the cloth-making process. Children could mime the different processes and invite other children to guess what they are doing. Select only two or three pictures for the children to place in sequence.

Assessment opportunities

Can the children sequence the process in the correct order and explain what is happening in their sequence?

Opportunities for IT

Children could use a simple CD-ROM encyclopaedia and look for information on spinning and weaving in the past. This would introduce them to simple searching using a key word, or browsing the encyclopaedia by clicking on highlighted words to take them to another linked section.

Display ideas

Children can create a large display with pictures illustrating the different stages in the cloth-making process. Provide different wools for children to feel and to examine with a magnifying glass. You may like to display any spindles and clay weights that the children used.

Reference to photocopiable sheet

The photocopiable page 121 shows the different stages of the cloth-making process before the Industrial Revolution. The pictures show: sheep being sheared; carding the wool; spinning wool; weaving cloth; dyeing cloth; making up clothes.

DESIGNING COATS OF ARMS

To find out about the way of life in the past through a study of coats of arms.

†† *Whole class then individual.*

🕐 *Whole class 20 minutes; individual 20 minutes.*

Previous skills/knowledge needed

This activity will extend children's knowledge about medieval knights.

Key background information

It was difficult for individual knights to be recognised when they were dressed in full armour. In order to differentiate between them they began to carry their own personal patterns and emblems on their shields. These emblems were also embroidered on the knights' surcoats which were worn over their armour and became known as their 'coats of arms'. Rules about how the patterns were to be made and which colours could be used soon developed. The colours used all had special names and there were rules about how they could be applied. For example there were two metal colours, gold and silver, and five tinctures, blue, red, black, green and purple. A metal was always placed on a tincture or a tincture on a metal. Heralds recognised the different coats of arms and knew to whom they belonged.

Preparation

Before you commence work ask the children to look out for different badges and coats of arms in their environment. This will probably include a wide assortment. For example badges associated with different sporting clubs, town/city coat of arms, royal coats of arms and bus companies. Collect different examples of coats of arms.

Resources needed

Pictures of different coats of arms. Pencils, crayons, felt-tipped pens.

What to do

Introduction

Discuss the children's findings. Talk about the variety of coats of arms and the different reasons why they have been designed. Do they tell us anything about the person or organisation to whom they belong?

Development

Tell the children that some of the first coat of arms were worn by knights in the past. Ask them to think of reasons why coats of arms might have been made. Using the background information talk about why coats of arms were important and describe how they were originally designed. Ask the children what symbols they would include on their own coat of arms. Suggestions might include some reference to their hobbies and interests, pets or their names. Ask the children to design their own coat of arms (you may need to provide an outline for them to complete). Encourage them to use the correct heraldic colours.

Suggestion(s) for extension

Encourage children to investigate the different places where coats of arms might be found for example stained glass windows; tombs; carvings on the sides of buildings; within paintings. Ask the children to look for pictures of the royal coats of arms and to copy them.

Assessment opportunities

Can the children explain why coats of arms were important in the past? Can children identify places where coats of arms may be found?

Opportunities for IT

Children could use an art package to design their own coat of arms. They could make the original design away from the computer and then use the computer to draw and edit the design. Show them how to make and draw lines of different thicknesses, draw different shapes such as circles and squares and then add and change colours. You could set up a file with an empty shield on it for the children to complete. Some art or drawing packages also allow children to use clip art within their design.

Display ideas

Draw around the outlines of the coat of arms in thick black crayon. Pour a little vegetable oil on to a ball of cotton wool and wipe it over the back of the design. When dry, stick the paper on the windows to create a stained glass effect.

A SURPRISE PIE

To identify differences between ways of life at different times. To identify different ways in which the past is represented; songs.

†† *Whole class then individuals.*

🕐 *Whole class 25 minutes; individuals 15 minutes.*

Previous skills/knowledge needed

This activity draws on children's knowledge of the nursery rhyme, *Sing a Song of Sixpence*.

Key background information

Medieval banquets were elaborate and governed by many rules such as where people should sit, how they should behave and what they should eat. The most important people at a banquet sat on a raised platform at the end of the hall 'above the salt', which was placed in a decorated container. Guests sat at other tables according to their importance and were given different foods accordingly. The tables were laid with cloths, knives, salt cellars and trenchers (thick slices of bread to act as plates), before the food was served. Hands were washed at the table in bowls of scented water. All the food and drink which was served to the nobles was tasted first to ensure that it was not poisoned or bad. Jugglers, acrobats and minstrels would entertain the guests as they were eating.

Swans and peacocks were served stuffed and placed on the table complete with their feathers. Boars heads were elaborately decorated. Sweets and pastries were made into different shapes, sometimes life-sized wild animals. There was a wide range of different meats: venison; beef; mutton; veal and rabbits. A variety of birds: chickens; pheasants; herons; partridge; woodcock and plover were also served. Fish such as salmon, pike, bream, trout, crabs, eels and shrimps were regularly eaten.

An occasional dish was a surprise pie. When they were cut open, live birds or frogs would spring out! Jellies and custards were served coloured with red, green, yellow or purple plant dyes.

Poor people's diet by comparison was very plain and monotonous. Vegetable soups, beans, pease pottage (thick paste of mashed peas), bacon, cheese and bread were staple foods.

Preparation

Gather together some household items such as a tablecloth and cutlery to set the scene.

Resources needed

Pictures and books about medieval ways of life. Colouring materials, pencils, tablecloth, knives, bowl filled with scented water. Thick slices of brown bread. Decorated container for the salt.

What to do

Introduction

Discuss with the children the different foods which are eaten at celebrations today. Explain that this activity looks at food in medieval times, which was the time when a lot of castles, which we can still see today, were built and lived in.

Development

Tell the children that in medieval times people marked special occasions with banquets and special food. Ask them if they think medieval people would eat the same foods as we eat today. Use the background information and explain to the children that they are going to help tell the story of a medieval banquet. Select some children to be cooks and ask them to mime the food preparation as you tell them what they had to prepare. Choose some other children to act as stewards, to lay the cloth, place the salt, knives, thick pieces of bread and bowls of scented water on the table. Other children can be chosen as guests and they can pretend to eat the various dishes, as you describe them. At the end of the banquet, the 'surprise pie' can be brought in and comments made on its contents. A final group of children could provide the entertainment at the end of the banquet by pretending to be jugglers, singers and acrobats.

Conclusion

Sing the nursery rhyme, *Sing a Song of Sixpence*. What did the cooks put in that surprise pie? Ask the children what they would choose to put in a surprise pie. Ask them to draw a picture of a large open pie and to show the pie's contents emerging. Ask the children if *Sing a Song of Sixpence* gives a lot of information about medieval banquets. What doesn't it tell them?

Suggestion(s) for extension

Children might like to further research rich medieval people's food. They could draw the food which was eaten on an outline of a table. They could contrast this food with the food eaten by poor people and draw a poor person's table too.

Opportunities for IT

Children could use a word processor to write their own version of the ingredients of the surprise pie. Try to organise this so the children can originate their text on the computer rather than entering their hand written versions. One way to achieve this might be for the children to work in small groups, so that they share the typing, or have an adult to act as a scribe, allowing them to concentrate on their ideas.

An alternative would be to make a class poem where pairs of children could come to the computer and add just one or two lines to the surprise pie ingredients. The final poem could be printed out for display in the classroom. As this may take some time children should be taught how to save and retrieve the poem as it grows to ensure they don't lose their work at the end of the day.

Display ideas

Make a giant surprise pie for a large wall frieze. Label the frieze with the words of *Sing a Song of Sixpence*. Children can make their own blackbirds with painted bodies and paper folded wings. Make stuffed swans or peacocks, using cut out children's painted handprints to represent the feathers. Make some of the foods for a medieval banquet from play dough and provide materials so that children can have their own medieval banquet in the play area.

MAKING FLOUR

To learn how flour was made in the past and to investigate how mills have developed over time.
†† *Whole class; then individuals.*
🕐 *Whole class 20 minutes; individuals variable.*

Previous skills/knowledge needed

Some experience of making models using construction or reclaimed materials. This activity could follow on from 'Growing corn' on page 63.

Key background information

Flour was first made by crushing grain between two stones. A smaller stone was rolled over a larger flat stone. It was a very long and tiring process. Later, circular stones called querns were used. Grain was poured into a central hole and crushed between two circular stones which were turned by a handle.

Wind and water power were later harnessed to turn larger

grinding stones. Windmills were sited on higher land to be able to make maximum use of the prevailing winds. Windmills and watermills were able to deal with much larger amounts of grain than the hand held querns and were in use right up until this century.

In the past the miller was an important member of the community, although not everybody liked to take their grain to him, since there were often tales of the miller keeping a bit of the flour back for himself!

Preparation

Obtain some corn (available from a farmer, mill, seed merchant or pet shop). Find some suitable flat stones which children can hold and use these to crush the corn together.

Resources needed

A collection of different flours: wholemeal; plain white; chapatti; granary and rice. Magnifying glasses, corn, flat stones. Construction and reclaimed materials. Adhesive, scissors. Pictures of old handmills, windmills and water mills.

What to do

Talk about the different flours which are available today. Use the magnifying glasses so the children can look closely at the different flours and ask them to describe them. Discuss with the children how flour is made from the corn. Ask the children to try crushing some of the corn together to make flour. Explain that this was the earliest way that flour was obtained. Was this an efficient method? Can the children think of any other ways to obtain flour? Talk about the earliest ways used to grind flour by hand. Explain how windmills and water mills could turn larger stones and consequently could grind more corn into flour. Can the children think of good locations for windmills and watermills? Look at some of the pictures of the different

mills from the resources. Using construction or reclaimed materials ask the children to build a model of a water or windmill which could be used for grinding corn.

Suggestion(s) for extension

Children can investigate the mechanism inside the windmill. They could draw the big stones used to grind the flour and stick their drawing inside the model of their windmill. Cut out the door of the windmill so that the drawing can be seen. Use a cog board to investigate how cogs work or make your own simple cogs from circular boxes edged with corrugated paper.

Suggestion(s) for support

Talk about what made the wheels inside the mills turn. Provide opportunities for children to play with water mills in the water tray and to make their own paper windmills which can be turned by the wind.

Assessment opportunities

Can the children describe how mills work and describe their development from the hand-held stones? Are the children able to explain why windmills and water mills were important in the past?

Opportunities for IT

Children could use a simple CD-ROM encyclopaedia to find out more about windmills or the way that flour was made in the past.

Display ideas

Display the children's models alongside the different flours. Invite the children to try to make their own flour using the stones and corn which are part of the display.

LEARNING TO WRITE AT SCHOOL

Using different sources to investigate ways in which children learned to write.

†† *Whole class then individual.*

⊕ *Whole class 20 minutes; individual 30 minutes.*

Previous skills/knowledge needed

Children will need to draw on their knowledge of hand-writing activities.

Key background information

In Victorian schools children began learning to write by doing pot hooks, which were lines with hooks at the top or loops at the bottom. Children copied these repeatedly in their sand trays using their fingers or sticks and rubbed them out by shaking the sand. Later children would have slates to practise their pot hooks and letters. The slate pencil often made a squeaking sound and the letters were rubbed off with a sponge or cloth. Only older children were allowed to use ink. Little ink-wells were filled from a large inkpot and children used pens with steel nibs and wooden holders to write in their copybooks. Good handwriting was regarded as very important (before the widespread use of the typewriter) and children would spend several hours a week practising. The phrases which the children had to copy out were often concerned with moral education and for imparting Christian values. Pencils were expensive and were generally reserved for drawing only.

Preparation

Prepare enough of the photocopiable sheet on page 122 for each child. Make a sand tray by filling a small tray with a thin layer of sand. Make enough books, 'My writing book' for the children in the class. (Alternatively, children may choose to stick the pictures in their topic books).

Resources needed

Photocopiable sheet (page 122), pencils, colouring materials, adhesive, scissors. A collection of writing materials; some sand poured into a deep tray; a slate and slate pencil; pens and washable ink; lined paper; blotting paper and pen wipes.

What to do
Introduction

Begin by discussing with the class the ways children are learning to write at the moment. How do they learn to form different letters? What writing implements do they use and where do they do their writing?

Development

Tell the children they are going to find out about how children learned to write in the past. Show the children the collection

of writing materials which you have assembled. Let the children try writing some letters in the sand tray and using the slate with the pencil. Ask the children why they think young children learned to write with sand trays and slates instead of paper and pencils. Hand out the photocopiable sheet to each child and look at the different writing materials which are illustrated. Talk about the time children spent copywriting and, at that time, the importance of good handwriting. Why were only the older children allowed to use ink? Talk about how the pens were used by carefully dipping them into the inkwell. Explain why the blotting paper and ink wipes were needed.

Conclusion

Ask the children to cut out the pictures on the photocopiable sheet and to stick them into 'My writing book'. They can draw a picture of themselves 'writing' now on the final page. Children might choose to draw themselves actually writing by hand in their writing book or working at a computer keyboard. Leave space beneath each picture for the children to label the picture and to describe how the different materials were/are used.

Suggestion(s) for extension

Children could experiment copywriting with dip-in pens and washable ink. This can be a messy activity so a supply of blotting paper and pen wipes is a good idea! Children could also research other materials which children used to write with in the past. Ancient Greek and Roman children learned their letters by using small wooden tablets coated with darkened wax. They used a stylus of wood, bone or metal to scratch the letters into the wax.

Suggestion(s) for support

Encourage the children to try forming letters and pot hooks using the sand tray and slate. Encourage them to talk about how writing at school was different in the past compared with today.

Assessment opportunities

Can the children talk about some of the different ways which children used to learn to write in the past and comment on their effectiveness?

Opportunities for IT

Use a CD-ROM encyclopaedia with the children to search for information on different forms of writing, Egyptian, Greek and Russian.

You could also explore the different styles of fonts on the class computer; many now have a range of fonts. Children could print out the same sentences written in several fonts and decide which they prefer, and decide when a particular font would be used. It is also possible to use fonts which copy a cursive handwriting style and these could be compared with Victorian writing styles. Compile a class font book with different examples and children's comments about the different font styles included. Children could use it as a reference on other occasions when they are using a word processor and wish to change the font.

Display ideas

Display the different writing materials mentioned in the resources and create an interactive display where children can be invited to experiment using them. Surround the display with examples of children's current writing using different materials and papers, for example computer printouts, writing with felt-tipped pens; pencils or crayons. Include examples of the beginning stages of the writing process, together with examples from more advanced writers.

Reference to photocopiable sheet

The photocopiable page 122 shows a sand tray; slate with slate pencil; copy writing paper with lines, pen and ink.

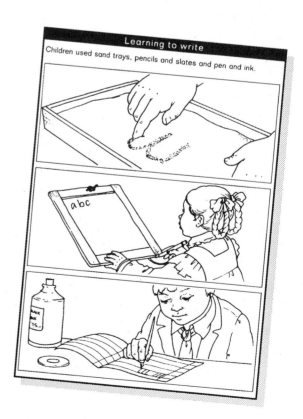

Learning to write
Children used sand trays, pencils and slates and pen and ink.

A VICTORIAN WASHDAY

To describe the laundry cycle in Victorian times and compare this with current practices. To draw conclusions about how time spent doing laundry might have affected ways of life in Victorian times.

†† *Whole group, then individuals.*

🕐 *20 minutes whole class; 20 minutes individuals.*

Previous skills/knowledge needed

Ability to join in discussion and to talk about the washing cycle at home.

Key background information

In Victorian times, washing, drying and ironing clothes was a long and laborious activity which would take all week. Traditionally Monday was washday. Water was heated in a large copper boiler or in kettles and saucepans over the fire and then poured into a dolly tub. Surface dirt would be scrubbed using a brush and bar of soap on a washboard. The washing would be sorted into white and coloured items. Whites would then be plunged into the hot water in the copper or dolly tub. A stick was used to stir the washing around. Coloured garments went into the copper or tub afterwards. A mangle was used to wring out the excess water before the washing was hung out to dry. Flat irons warmed by the fire were used for ironing. The washing was then aired on clothes horses beside the fire or on racks hanging above.

Preparation

Prepare photocopiable sheet on page 123 for each child.

▲ Draw pictures or write about what happens to your washing today.

Resources needed

Pictures and books which illustrate and provide information about doing the washing now and in the past. A selection of washing artefacts: a dolly tub; scrubbing board; bar of soap; wooden scrubbing brush and box of soap powder .Pencils and crayons, photocopiable sheet page 123.

What to do

Introduction

Talk about doing the washing today. Do the children's families wash at home or the launderette? What machines are used? Is any washing done by hand? What makes the washing clean? Talk about hot water and types of washing powder and liquids. How is the washing dried, ironed and aired?

Development

Examine and talk about the Victorian washing artefacts if they are available. Alternatively, look at the pictures on the photocopiable sheet which illustrate artefacts used for washing in Victorian times. Compare washing in Victorian times with what happens today, drawing attention to the use of machines as opposed to manual work.

Conclusion

Ask the children to complete the photocopiable sheet by drawing modern equivalents of each washing artefact and writing about them.

Suggestion(s) for extension

Use the photocopiable sheet and other resources to write out a list of instructions for doing the laundry in Victorian times. Children could also research washing practices in earlier times.

Suggestion(s) for support

Draw or cut out from magazines pictures of appliances and machines which are used for doing the washing today. Some children might find the spaces too small on the photocopiable sheets for their drawings of current washing artefacts. Provide larger pieces of paper for these children to draw their artefacts.

Assessment opportunities

Can the children recognise differences between the past and present ways of laundering clothes? Can they talk about how the long, laborious washing process might have affected women's lives in the past?

Opportunities for IT

Children could make their own list of instructions for doing the washing in Victorian times, using a word processor to help them order the instructions. Show the children the ways that text can be moved around the screen, either using a 'cut and paste' approach, where the text is deleted from the page and then pasted back in at the new position, or a 'drop and drag' facility which enables children to mark a section of text and then drag it to the new position using the mouse.

Younger children could use a concept keyboard linked to a word processor to sequence the wash day process. The concept keyboard overlay could have either pictures of the different parts of the washing process or sentences describing it, or both. By pressing on the relevant picture or sentence the word can be written onto the computer screen and then printed out.

Children could do the same for a modern wash day, and notice the difference in the number of instructions, or the amount of time taken.

Display ideas

Children can add their own pictures and writing to a 'then-and-now' display, illustrating changes in laundering clothes.

Reference to photocopiable sheet

The photocopiable sheet on page 123 shows a posset stick beside a dolly tub; a mangle; clothes hanging on a washing line; a woman ironing clothes with a flat iron.

CLOCKS AND TELLING THE TIME

To extend their awareness of the importance of recording time and to investigate different time-keeping devices from the past.

†† *Whole class introduction and development; individuals or pairs; working in groups conclusion.*

⏱ *Introduction 25 minutes; development 25 minutes; conclusion variable.*

Previous skills/knowledge needed

Some background knowledge of clocks and their purpose would be helpful.

Key background information

Keeping accurate time has only been important in the last two hundred years. Standardised national time came along with the advent of the railways and their timetables from the 1830s onwards.

The earliest clocks were probably shadow clocks which relied on the sun. Ancient Egyptians used simple shadow clocks and also built large obelisks which cast their shadows in a circle marked on the ground. The Ancient Egyptians were also familiar with water clocks made from pottery bowls with the hours marked off inside the bowl. Sand clocks worked on similar principles to the water clocks, and hours were measured as the sand trickled through a small hole. Sand glasses came into use about 1,200 years ago. To keep the sand perfectly dry it was enclosed within a glass container. In the middle, the neck of the sandglass narrowed so that the sand trickled through more slowly. Glasses were made in a variety of sizes so that different periods of time could be measured. They were taken on long sea voyages to estimate the speed at which the ship was travelling.

Candle clocks are said to have been invented by King Alfred. They had lines marked at intervals to show how many hours had passed as the candle burned. Other candle clocks had alternating layers of different coloured wax to mark off the passage of the hours. Fire clocks were used by the Chinese and were sometimes used as alarm clocks. The clocks were made from a mixture of sawdust and clay sticks which burned slowly. At certain intervals, threads holding up copper or brass weights were suspended near the sticks. When the sticks burned through the threads the weights fell down and were meant to act as an alarm. Long ago, few people owned clocks themselves. They probably learned what time it was by listening to the loud chimes of the town bell, struck by a man who was expected to ring it every hour.

The first clocks (fourteenth century) did not have a clock face or moving hands; they were made with metal figures of men striking the hours on the bell. The first household clocks were made in the late 1300s or early 1400s. They were made

of iron and had only one hand. Weights hung below the clock attached to ropes or chains which could be used for raising the weights up after they had dropped. In the seventeenth century the use of the pendulum enabled clocks to keep more accurate time since the pendulum controlled the speed of the moving parts within the clock. Long case clocks (grandfather clocks) provided enough room for the pendulum to swing, however they took up a lot of space. Smaller table clocks were invented; they had a small pendulum and were worked by a spring instead of weights. The spring was wound into a tight coil which as it unwound, worked the wheels on the clock to show the time.

Preparation
Prepare tables ready for model-making.

Resources needed
Pictures of different types of clocks and time keeping devices from books, magazines and posters. Reclaimed materials suitable for making model clocks, adhesive, scissors, adhesive tape, sand, construction materials, paper, pencils.

What to do
Introduction
Discuss with the children why we need to know the time. Why is it important? On what occasions do we need to know the time? Make a list of times it is important to know about for example starting school; watching a television programme; knowing when a shop will be open; keeping an appointment to see the doctor or the dentist. Explain to the children that a long time ago most people did not have clocks. Look at the list which you have created about important times. In the past, would people have needed to know these times? If they did, how do the children think they would have managed?
Development
Ask the children to look around the locality and their homes and to note the different time-keeping devices which they can see. Encourage the children to describe some of the devices which they have seen. Talk about the different types for example, alarm clocks, church clocks, grandfather clocks, watches, clocks on ovens and egg timers. Discuss different ways of recording the passage of time such as clock faces and digital times. Use the background information to talk with the children about the different ways of telling the time in the past. Refer to any pictures or books from your resources.

Conclusion
Organise children into groups to make their own models of different time-keeping devices from reclaimed or construction materials. Ask the children to draw a diagram of the model which they intend to make. What materials will they need for their model? Collect the materials together. Alternatively some children might like to make their models from construction materials. Different groups could make: shadow clocks or sundials, sand and water clocks, long case clocks, candle clocks. When they have been completed ask the children to write a label for their clock describing how it works.

Suggestion(s) for extension
The activity can be extended to encourage children to make more accurate time keeping devices. For example can they make a sand or water clock which will measure five minutes duration? Can they make a shadow clock in the playground to mark off the hours of the school day?

Suggestion(s) for support
Children may need support in using appropriate vocabulary and phrases to talk about time. The time-keeping models can be adapted to suit children's different abilities and stages of maturity. Children can suggest appropriate labels for their models which can be written out by an adult.

Assessment opportunities
Do the children recognise why knowing the time can be important now and can they contrast this with people's knowledge of accurate time in the past? Can children describe different methods used for recording time?

Opportunities for IT
If children make a shadow clock they could use graphing software to produce a bar chart of the shadow lengths at hourly intervals during the day.

Children could also use a simple encyclopaedia CD-ROM to look for information on clocks. This would introduce them to simple searches using key words or how to browse a CD-ROM using the highlighted words which link various pages together. Provide some simple questions to start, and then give some more open ended questions which could include some key words which they could use to make a search.

A simple question might be 'what is a water clock?' where children search for the words *water clock*. A more taxing question might be 'how did the Romans tell the time?' Children could be asked to make up questions for others to answer at a later date. It is, of course, important to check that the information is on your CD-ROM before you start!

Display ideas
Display the model clocks with their labels explaining how they work. Children might like to design a collage of different clocks and time-keeping devices for a background display. They could draw their own pictures and also cut out pictures from magazines and catalogues to add to the collage.

LIGHTING HOMES IN THE PAST

To compare current forms of lighting with those used in the past. To discuss how lighting might have affected different people's lives in the past.

†† *Group and then pairs.*

🕐 *20 minutes group; 30 minutes pairs.*

Previous skills/ knowledge needed
Children will need to draw on their knowledge about sources of light in their own homes.

Key background information
The photocopiable sheet on page 124 shows different forms of lighting that were used in the past. Roman pottery lamps were filled with olive oil. Wax candles were expensive and poorer families made do with home-made rushlights, made from rushes dipped in animal fat. In Victorian times, oil lamps and candles were used. Gas lamps which were fitted to the wall were also a popular source of lighting. Electric light bulbs were patented in 1878, but were only used by the rich who could afford generators. Children should also become aware that poor artificial lighting encouraged people to make the best use of natural light, rising early and going to bed early.

Preparation
Organise a collection of different light sources. Photocopy the worksheet on page 124 so that you have one sheet per pair of children.

Resources needed
A collection of different objects which provide light, for example, torches, various candles, an oil lamp, a lantern, children's night lights and luminous plugs, pictures of different forms of lighting, photocopiable sheet on page 124, pencils, crayons, felt-tipped pens, scissors, adhesive.

What to do
Introduction
Discuss with the children the different sorts of lighting which they have in their own homes and ask them to describe them. Encourage the children to handle the objects in the display if they are safe, and look at the pictures. Describe the objects and encourage the children to talk about how they are used. Ask the children to sort the objects into different groups. Encourage them to find different ways of grouping the lights and discuss reasons for their grouping. For example, some groupings which the children might suggest are: lights which can be carried around, lights which belong in the bedroom/ sitting rooms, lights which were used in the past.

Development
Talk about what makes particular lights work for example electricity, or oil. Encourage the children to sort the objects and pictures into different sources of power. Discuss together which lights would give the best light and then ask the children to group the lights into: very bright; bright and dim.

Conclusion
Ask the children to look at the pictures on the photocopiable sheet and, in pairs, talk about the different forms of lighting used in the past. Ask the children to draw lines to match the names to the lights. Children can then cut out the pictures and working in pairs, sort them into different groups. Encourage the children to find different ways of sorting their pictures, referring back to the earlier group discussion.

Suggestion(s) for extension
Ask the children to try placing the different lights in a sequence to form a light timeline. They can then use books and pictures for reference to draw and label other lights which were used in the past and write about them.

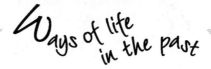
Suggestion(s) for support

Children might need help reading the labels and attaching the correct labels to the appropriate pictures. Alternatively, the labelling activity can be omitted and the children can simply use the pictures to sort and group.

Assessment opportunities

Listen carefully to how the children talk about the past. What vocabulary and phrases do they use? For example: long ago; in the past; when my mum was little. Can they talk about how ways of life might have been affected through using different sorts of light? For example: going to bed earlier; ensuring safety with candles.

Opportunities for IT

Children could use a word processor to write labels for the display of lights. Children could write a simple guide to the display using a word processor, or a simple desktop publishing package. This could highlight just a few of the items on display. The tasks could be shared around the group with each child in the group selecting and writing about one type of light.

Prepare a format for the guide in advance with each child given an allotted space for their writing. A simple booklet format could be used which provided a space for each child in the group to write a little about the light they have chosen and add an illustration which can be added by hand later, or, if the school has a scanner added electronically on the word processed page. If children have access to a colour printer they can also experiment with colour to make their guide more attractive.

Display ideas

Use the resources gathered to create a display about lighting. Use questions to focus children's attention on the sources of power and the effectiveness of different lights. Ask: What lights do we use in our homes? What lights did people have in the past? Which objects give the brightest lights?

Which candle gives the best light?

Lighting homes
▲ Draw lines to match the names to the lights.

bedside lamp
electric striplight
rush light
Roman lamp
gas lamp
oil lamp
candle
torch

Reference to photocopiable sheet

Photocopiable page 124 shows different sources of light: a Roman lamp; a rush light; a candle; a gas lamp; a Victorian oil lamp; bedside lamp; torch; electric strip light.

SUPPLYING WATER TO THE HOME

To compare water supplies to homes in the past with present day supplies. To draw conclusions about the effects of water supply on people's lives in the past.

†† *Whole group and then individuals.*

🕐 *25 minutes whole group; 10 minutes individuals.*

Previous skills/knowledge needed

This activity will draw on children's knowledge of the supply of water to their own homes.

Key background information

Before mains water was supplied to houses people were dependent on wells and pumps for their daily needs. Water carriers sold fresh water. All the water had to be carried to where it was needed. Water was precious and used sparingly. In Victorian times poor families would use the same water to wash clothes, crockery, children and floors. Fresh, clean water was not always available and was rarely drunk. Adults and children preferred to drink ale or weak beer instead. Poor

people were often dependant on a communal pipe, standing at the end of the street and shared by many families. The water was turned on for a limited period each day and people rushed to collect their ration. Wealthier families installed water taps in their own homes. In Victorian times diseases originating from polluted water supplies such as cholera were common in towns and cities. Drains emptied out into rivers which supplied water; sewage often contaminated the water supply.

Preparation

Before you begin work in class, walk around school and note the places where water is supplied. Next, ask the children to note where water is supplied in their own home for example kitchen taps, washing machine, bathroom, shower, garden taps. Talk about reservoirs storing water which is then piped to our own homes. Prepare the photocopiable sheet on page 125 for each child.

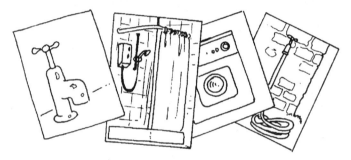

Resources needed

Books and pictures of different sources of water for example pumps, wells, streams, reservoirs. Pencils, crayons, felt-tipped pens, a large bucket filled with water, cloths or newspapers for mopping up spilled water, photocopiable page 125.

What to do

Introduction

Remind the children about how water is stored and brought to our homes today. Introduce the idea that in the past there was no mains water and no pipes and taps in the home.

Development

Ask the children to suggest where they think people might have obtained water. It might help the children to refer to some well known nursery rhymes such as, *Jack and Jill went up the hill to fetch a pail of water*, or *Ding dong bell, pussy's in the well*. Encourage the children to practise miming collecting water from a well or pumping water into a bucket from an iron pump as they sing these rhymes. Emphasise that water had to be carried to wherever it was needed. Fill up a large bucket of water and ask the children to carry it. Is it too heavy? Can they carry it very far?

Conclusion

Hand out the photocopiable sheets to each child and together look at the pictures and use them as a basis for talking about how water reached homes in the past. Discuss the quality

of the water and how far the water would have to be carried home. How do the children think people would have managed for water if it had not rained for a long time? Encourage the children to draw comparisons between current water supplies and those in the past. How might difficulties in obtaining good, clean water have affected people's lives in the past? Consider the time spent collecting supplies; having to save water from different tasks – clothes washing water could be used to wash the floor; diseases occurring through the use of dirty water supplies.

Finish by asking the children to label the pictures on the photocopiable sheet.

Suggestion(s) for extension

Some children may be able to estimate how many bucketfuls of water they would need to collect in a day for their needs. How many trips to a well or pump would they need to make? They could estimate how long this would take.

Suggestion(s) for support

Some children may need help with reading and labelling the pictures on the photocopiable sheet. The sheet can be used as a source of information and the children could be asked to draw their own pictures of water supplies in the past on larger pieces of paper.

Assessment opportunities

Can children talk about some of the differences in supplying water to homes in the past? Can they explain how lack of mains water and a good, clean water supply might have affected people's lives in the past?

Water in the home
▲ Match the label to the pictures.

rainwater tub
pump
stand pipe
stream
well
water seller

Opportunities for IT

Children could work out how much water they needed in a day. Set up a simple matrix to record information:

▲ water for drinking;

▲ water for washing;

▲ water for washing clothes;

▲ water for cleaning teeth;

▲ water for the toilet.

They could then undertake simple measuring activities to work out how much is used and then use graphing software to record the results for each category. They could then print out a bar or pie chart and describe what their results show. They could also work out how many buckets of water would be needed in a day.

Display ideas

Children can make their own models of wells and pumps. They could try making a yoke to fit across a doll's shoulders which could balance two paper cups.

Reference to photocopiable sheet

The photocopiable sheet on page 125 shows pictures of a pump; well; rainwater tub to catch water draining from the roof; stream; a water seller with a yoke and two buckets of water; a stand pipe in a Victorian slum.

INSIDE A VICTORIAN KITCHEN

To learn about kitchens in Victorian times and to contrast this with kitchens today. To draw conclusions about life in Victorian times.

†† *Whole class introductory activity dependent on the amount of information collected.*

⊕ *Paired discussion 10 minutes; whole class concluding discussion 10 minutes; model making in pairs or individually, variable amount of time required.*

Previous skills/knowledge needed

Ability to join in discussion and talk about kitchens in their own home.

Key background information

Victorian kitchens in wealthy and middle-class households were dominated by the cooking range which had to be cleaned out and lit on a daily basis. The fire from the range heated different hobs and ovens. The range had to be cleaned regularly with a special black polish called 'black lead'. The kitchens remained warm due to the fire so any food that was perishable was stored on cold slabs or in safes in different rooms such as a pantry, larder or cellar. Washing-up and vegetable preparation were generally undertaken in the scullery which could also serve as a laundry room. Sometimes the laundry was done in a separate outhouse.

Preparation

Prepare the photocopiable sheet on page 126, one per pair of children.

Resources needed

Pictures and books about Victorian homes and kitchens, photocopiable page 126, writing materials for the teacher, reclaimed materials and other materials for model making, adhesive and scissors.

What to do

Introduction

Ask the children to make a plan of their kitchen at home, noting the appliances and utensils and what they are used for. Collect and display data on the different sorts of appliances. For example: numbers of households which have a gas or electric cooker; or with microwaves/toasters/fridges. This needs handling sensitively with regard to individual family circumstances of the children in the class.

Development

Ask the children which appliances and utensils they would expect to find in a kitchen a hundred years ago? Give each pair of children a copy of the photocopiable sheet on page 126 of a Victorian kitchen and ask them to note the different objects which they can see. Are there any similarities or differences with modern kitchens? Once children have discussed the picture, gather them together to discuss their findings as a class. Together make a list of things which are the same and things which are different. Talk about what it would have been like to have worked in a Victorian kitchen.

Conclusion

Use the photocopiable sheet and any other sources of information for the children to create their own models of a Victorian kitchen. Use shoe boxes to create a model of a kitchen, and a Victorian range could be created from several small boxes.

Suggestion(s) for extension
Children can conduct their own research to find out more about Victorian kitchens using other reference materials. They could write a diary account of somebody working in the kitchen. Children might also be interested in researching kitchens in other periods of the past.

Suggestion(s) for support
Encourage the children to look carefully at the picture of the Victorian kitchen and to identify and explain at least one difference which they can see.

Assessment opportunities
Can the children identify differences between their own and Victorian kitchens? Can they explain how these differences might have affected how people lived in the past? For example, the importance of keeping the fire in the range burning; the time it took for the food to be cooked. Are the children able to use the sources of information as evidence to accurately reconstruct their own Victorian kitchens?

A Victorian kitchen

Opportunities for IT
Children could make a simple database about kitchens, selecting a few of the most important kitchen appliances or tools. Each record of the database could contain:

Name of child	Gurdeep
Cooker	gas
Microwave	yes
Washing machine	yes
Tumble dryer	no

Children could collect the information on a simple data collection sheet and then take it in turns to come to the computer and type their information into a database set up in advance by the teacher. Once all the data has been entered children can answer simple questions such as: How many homes cook by gas?; Which sort of cooker is the most popular, gas or electricity?; How many homes do not have a tumble dryer?

This could lead to comparisons and discussions about how Victorian people cooked, or dried their washing. The data can also be represented in graphical format using bar or pie charts.

Children could also use a CD-ROM to look for information about kitchens, past and present. They might also be able to use photographic material taken from a CD-ROM to look at other aspects of Victorian kitchens.

Display ideas
Create a model of a kitchen in the classroom play area. Build the range from empty cardboard boxes and cut some of the boxes so that they can open as oven doors. Place a kettle and pans on the hobs. Paint a fire in the grate. Make your own coal from painted crumpled newspaper and store it in a coal scuttle. Build a mantlepiece and decide what to place on it. Add a dresser, children might like to make their own Victorian plates from papier mâché.

Reference to the photocopiable sheet
The photocopiable page 126 illustrates a kitchen in a middle-class Victorian home. Items to note are the kitchen range with different hobs and ovens. The long-handled saucepans are on the hobs and a flat iron is on top of the oven. Beside the range is a coal scuttle and some bellows. A toasting fork hangs beside the fire. A lace cloth covers the mantelpiece which is decorated with ornaments and also has candlesticks which are used for lighting upstairs. Above the fire is a clothes-rack hanging from the ceiling to dry clothes. The room is lit by gas lighting. On the floor is a home-made rag rug and there is a carpet beater. A dresser with various pots and plates stands in one corner. At the table in the centre of the room someone is making bread and the tins are ready to be put into the oven.

A KITCHEN TIMELINE

To learn about different kitchens in the past and ways of cooking food. To compare kitchens across different periods of time and to arrange pictures of kitchens in chronological order.

†† *Whole class introduction, followed by pairs/ individual.*

🕐 *Whole class 20 minutes; pairs/individuals 30 minutes.*

A kitchen timeline
▲ Cut out the pictures and put them in order. Begin with the oldest.

Previous skills/knowledge needed

This activity will draw on children's knowledge of different ways of cooking food.

Key background information

In the Viking house there was no separate kitchen; the occupants lived entirely in one room. The open fireplace in the centre of the room provided both heat and a means for cooking food.

By Tudor times some large farmhouses would have had a separate room as a kitchen. Food was still cooked over an open fire, with meats being roasted on long metal rods, called spits. Cauldrons used for boiling meat and vegetables were hung on pot cranes. The pot crane could be used to swing the cauldron over the hottest part of the fire or to the edge if slower cooking was required. A ratchet enabled the pot to be raised up and down above the fire. Most animals were killed in the autumn and their meat was salted or smoked over the fire to preserve it. Bake-ovens were often built into Tudor fireplaces. Before baking started, a bundle of dry sticks was put in the oven and set alight. When the oven was hot enough, the ashes were raked out and the bread, pies and pastries were put inside, using a flat long handled shovel.

The coal fire in the Victorian range heated different ovens and hobs. Various devices were used to regulate the temperature inside the different ovens. Not all families could afford these cooking stoves and many still cooked over open fires or sent their food to the 'bakehouse' to be cooked. See page 50 for further information on the Victorian kitchen.

Preparation

Prepare the photocopiable sheet on page 127 for each child. Cut strips of paper or card for each child to make a timeline.

Resources needed

Pictures of different kitchens in the past, photocopiable sheet on page 127, pencils and colouring materials, scissors, adhesive, paper or card.

What to do

Introduction

Talk about all the different types of foods that are eaten today and the different methods of cooking them, for example boiling, roasting, baking, steaming and frying. Discuss the different appliances and equipment used in modern kitchens such as microwaves, electric/gas cookers, toasters, saucepans, frying pans and so on.

Development

Hand out the photocopiable sheet to each child and talk about what can be seen in the pictures. Refer to additional picture resources if available. Look at how food was cooked and what utensils were used in each scene on the photocopiable page. Individually or in pairs, ask the children to cut out the pictures and sequence them from the oldest to the most recent. Encourage the children to give reasons for their sequence and provide opportunities for them to make suggestions as to what life would have been like working in the different kitchens.

Conclusion

Children can draw a picture of their own kitchen on a separate piece of paper. The pictures can be glued onto paper or card to complete a timeline.

Suggestion(s) for extension

Ask the children to describe some of the jobs that had to be done in the different kitchens, for example gathering the firewood; turning the spit; raking out the grate for cinders. Using found or construction materials ask the children to try to make a working model of a cooking spit which turns to roast the meat evenly.

Suggestion(s) for support

Some children might need help identifying features in older kitchens. Talk with the children and guide them with clues which they can use to help organise their sequence.

Assessment opportunities

Can the children describe how the kitchens have changed over periods of time? Can they note any similarities or differences between the kitchens?

Opportunities for IT

Children could use a word processor to write labels and descriptions of the key parts of the different kitchen pictures. Mount the pictures on the wall and use the labels to link to the relevant part of the picture, for example the pot crane in a Tudor kitchen or the range in a Victorian kitchen.

Display ideas

Use the information from the photocopiable sheet and additional resources to create large friezes of different kitchens in the past. Label the displays to encourage children to compare the different features in the kitchens.

Reference to photocopiable sheet

The photocopiable page 127 shows the interior of a Viking house, with a central fireplace edged with stones. Points to note are the hearth cakes being baked on hot stones by the fire and the large cauldron containing a vegetable stew. The Tudor farmhouse kitchen has a large fireplace with meat being roasted on a spit and a cauldron hanging over the fire from a pot crane. On one side of the fireplace a bake oven has been built into the wall. The Victorian kitchen has a range with different hobs and ovens for cooking different dishes.

LONDON BRIDGE IS FALLING DOWN

To learn about an important building and to experience how it has been remembered through songs and rhymes.

†† *Whole class.*

🕐 *30 minutes.*

Previous skills/knowledge needed

Children will need to be familiar with the traditional nursery rhyme *London Bridge is falling down*.

Key background information

Records of the song *London Bridge is falling down* having been sung go back to the seventeenth century and the time of Charles II. The song's first appearance in print dates from c1744, in the children's book, *Tommy Thumb's Pretty Song Book*. The port of London developed around the bridgehead which the Romans had established. In medieval times London Bridge was part of the busy port. In 1176 builders began work on a stone bridge to replace the old wooden bridge which had often been destroyed by fire or flood water. The stone bridge needed constant repair to withstand the currents beneath its arches. Along the top of the bridge there was a narrow roadway, with houses and shops on either side. Boatmen used to ferry people and goods across the river.

London Bridge remained the only bridge across the river Thames until Westminster Bridge was opened to traffic in 1750. Blackfriars Bridge was opened in 1769. The old houses and shops on London Bridge were eventually pulled down to make the roadway wider going across the bridge.

> London Bridge is falling down, falling down.
> London Bridge is falling down, falling down.
> My fair lady.
>
> Build it up with sticks and stones, sticks and stones.
> Sticks and stones will wear away, wear away...
>
> Build it up with iron and steel......
> Iron and steel will rust away......
>
> Build it up with bricks and clay......
> Bricks and clay will wash away .....
>
> Build it up with silver and gold ....
> Silver and gold is stole away.....
>
> Then we'll set a man to watch, man to watch.
> Then we'll set a man to watch,
> *My fair lady.*

Resources needed

Pictures of old London Bridge, showing the shops and houses on the bridge.

What to do

Begin by singing and playing the game, *London Bridge is Falling Down*. Two children can make an arch for other children to walk through. On the line, '*My fair lady*', the children forming the arch lower their arms and catch whoever is going through at the time. The child who is caught then has to stand behind one of the children making the arch, until all the children have been caught.

Using the background information tell the children why London Bridge has always been so important. If possible show a picture of the old London Bridge from your resources. Ask the children if they can think of any reasons why the bridge might fall down. Talk about the different materials used for building bridges. Which would be the strongest? What other materials can the children suggest?

Talk about how children have sung this song for hundreds of years and explain how the words have been passed down by people singing it together. Explain that it was only later that the words were written in books to remind people of the verses. Ask the children why they think a song was made up about London Bridge.

Suggestion(s) for extension

Children could think of other materials for building London Bridge and make up another verse for the song. Children can ask their parents and friends if they know any other versions. Different verses can be written down to show how differences might arise when people pass the words along by word of mouth.

Children could investigate other rhymes and songs associated with places, for example *Ride a cock horse to Banbury Cross*. Where is Banbury? What is the cross like? Was it an important feature?

Suggestion(s) for support

If necessary reduce the number of verses for the song.

Assessment opportunities

Can children think of reasons why London Bridge was an important building and why it was often in need of repair?

Display ideas

Children can contribute to a group model of old London Bridge. Some children can make the arches and roadway going across the river. Other children can construct a variety of timber-framed houses and shops to go on either side of the road.

BUILDING A CASTLE

To find out about aspects of the past from buildings and sites.

†† *Whole class then individuals/pairs.*

🕐 *Whole class 15 minutes; individuals/pairs variable.*

Previous skills/knowledge needed

Some experience of designing and making models.

Key background information

The first castles (motte and bailey castles) were built about nine hundred years ago. The motte was a mound of earth on which a wooden tower was built. This was the strongest part of the castle. The bailey was a yard enclosed by a wooden fence where the animals were kept. Stone was soon used to replace the wooden structures.

Later castles – concentric castles – had two sets of stone walls. In addition to the Lord and his family, a whole community would live inside the castle walls. For example, soldiers; servants; blacksmiths; armourers and carpenters.

Plentiful supplies of food and a good source of water were needed in case of siege. Enemies used several different methods to attack for example scaling ladders to climb over the walls; battering rams were used to crash against walls and break down the doors; heavy rocks were hurled over and against the walls by trebuchets and ballistas (similar to giant catapults). Sometimes tunnels were dug beneath the castles to weaken the foundations. Inside the castle, the barbican protected the main doorway which had a drawbridge and portcullis (slatted iron gate). Defenders fired arrows from the narrow slit windows and would drop hot ashes or sand, rocks and boiling water onto the attackers.

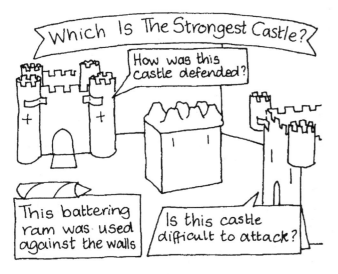

Which Is The Strongest Castle?

How was this castle defended?

This battering ram was used against the walls

Is this castle difficult to attack?

Preparation

A visit to a nearby castle would be a good starting point for this activity. Ask if any children have been inside a castle and encourage them to talk about their visit before starting the classwork.

Resources needed

Pictures/posters and books illustrating different sorts of castles. Card, scissors, adhesive and paints. Construction and reclaimed materials.

What to do

Look at the pictures of the castles together. Why do the children think castles were built? Talk about who lived there. Look at the features which made the castles safe places to be for example walls, moat, drawbridge, portcullis, narrow arrow slit windows. Talk about the ways in which castles were attacked and how the inhabitants protected themselves.

Ask the children to design their own castle taking into account some of these features. They will need to draw a plan and indicate what materials they will use. Using their plans, ask the children to construct their own castles from reclaimed or construction materials. Encourage the children to evaluate their designs carefully and to explain how their castle is defended.

Suggestion(s) for extension

Encourage children to design working parts for their castle. For example can they design a mechanism to lower and raise the drawbridge? Design a siege engine which could be used to attack a castle.

Suggestion(s) for support

Some children may need help in planning their castles and in translating their ideas into 3D models.

Assessment opportunities

Can the children identify safe places in the castle? Listen to the explanations they give as to why they were safe.

Opportunities for IT

Use a CD-ROM to search for pictures or information about castles. Show the children how to make a simple search using keywords or how to browse the CD-ROM using highlighted words on key pages. Children might also want to print out pictures of castles that they find and they will need to be shown how to do this, or supported with this work.

Children could also use framework software like *My World 2* with the 'Design a Castle' resources pack. The completed design can be printed out as a net with tabs for gluing the final model together.

Display ideas

Display the different castles and ask the children to make labels to show the different parts of their castle.

A RUINED CASTLE

To identify different ways in which the past is represented. To find out about aspects of the past from a range of sources of information; buildings and sites.

†† *Whole class then individuals.*

⏱ *Whole class 15 minutes; individuals 15 minutes.*

Previous skills/knowledge needed

Some knowledge of castles and why they were built. This activity can develop from 'Building a castle', page 54.

Key background information

Most medieval castles we can see today are now in ruins. Strong castle walls were ineffective against the widespread use of gunpowder and cannons in the fifteenth century. As the monarchy became more powerful, fewer nobles and lords fought against each other and kept their own armies. The countryside became more peaceful and nobles began to move out of their castles and to build large imposing country houses, which were more comfortable to live in.

Preparation

Prepare the photocopiable sheet on page 128 for each child. Collect pictures and books about castle life.

Resources needed

Pictures and books showing illustrations of life in medieval castles and photographs of castle ruins. Photocopiable sheet on page 128. Pencils, crayons and felt-tipped pens.

What to do

Ask the children how we know so much about castles. Look at some of the artists' impressions of castles and of medieval castle life from different books. Ask the children how the artists knew what to put in their pictures. Children may be

55

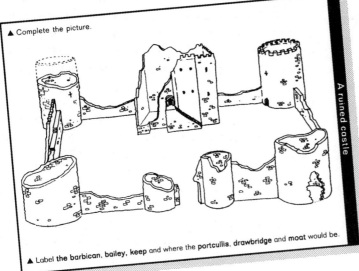

▲ Complete the picture.

A ruined castle

▲ Label the barbican, bailey, keep and where the portcullis, drawbridge and moat would be.

Suggestion(s) for support
Some children might find completing the castle difficult. Ask them instead to draw their own castle using pictures and books as sources of information.

Assessment opportunities
Can the children talk about how we know about castles? Do they know of any sources of information which tell us about castle life?

Opportunities for IT
Use a CD-ROM to search for pictures or information about castles. Show the children how to make a simple search using keywords or how to browse the CD-ROM using highlighted words on key pages. Children might also want to print out pictures of castles that they find and need to be shown how to do this, or supported with this work.

Reference to photocopiable sheet
The photocopiable sheet on page 128 shows the ruins of a castle which children can complete to show what the castle might have looked like when it was built. More able children can label the barbican (castle entrance), bailey (courtyard), keep (central tower) and indicate where the portcullis, drawbridge and moat would have been.

surprised by this question and this provides opportunities for discussion on sources of information. For example, castle ruins provide information about the size and structure of the building; pictures from medieval manuscripts provide information about what people wore and some of the things which they did; artefacts such as armour tell us what the knights wore. Artists use such sources of information to build up pictures of what life might have been like.

Hand out the photocopiable sheet of the castle ruins and talk about what can be seen in the picture. Ask the children to identify where the features of the castle, listed at the bottom of the sheet, are on the picture. Ask the children to complete the picture to show what the castle might have looked like when it had just been built. They can add vegetation and people around the castle to complete their picture.

Suggestion(s) for extension
Ask the children to label the different places on their castle, using the words at the bottom of the photocopiable sheet.

STREET TRADERS AND STREET CRIES

To learn about how goods were bought and sold in the past, by listening to traditional songs and rhymes and creating their own street cries.

†† *Whole class; individuals.*

🕐 *Whole class 20 minutes; individuals 20 minutes.*

Previous skills/knowledge needed
This activity requires the children to sing and to call out different street cries.

Key background information
Street traders were much more common in the past than today. There were fewer shops and people sold their produce in the street. Many children were street sellers, and in order to sell their wares they used 'street cries'. Some cries were seasonal and dependant on the availability of the produce. For example, walnuts 'Crack 'em! Try 'em before ye buy 'em!', apples 'Ripe apples of every size!' and pears 'Pears for pies!' in the autumn; cherries 'Round and sound. Two pence per pound!' and strawberries 'Ripe strawberries! Who buys my ripe straws?' in the summer. There was a wide range of foods

which could be offered for sale, including mackerel; salmon; new laid eggs; oysters; oranges and lemons; milk; watercress; rabbits; vinegar. Numerous articles were sold in the street and were accompanied by different cries from the vendors. 'Pins pretty maids pins! Buy pins pretty woman!' 'Buy a very fine mousetrap!' As well as food other goods sold this way included: walking sticks; singing birds such as linnets and larks kept in wooden cages; baskets and straw hats; lavender; coal; kindling wood; pots and pans, brushes and brooms.

Street criers could also offer particular services. The chimney sweep called; 'Sweep! Sweep! All the money I earn I keep! Sweep! Sweep!'; London bootblack boys called out, 'Shoe black your honour! Japan your shoes sir!' (Japan was a kind of black shoe polish). The knife and scissor grinder, the ratcatcher, and the mender of old pots and pans all had their different cries.

Preparation
Prepare the photocopiable sheet on page 129 for each child.

Resources needed
Photocopiable sheet on page 129. Scissors, colouring materials. Cassette player.

What to do
Introduction
Ask the children to think about goods which are sold in the street today and to make a note how sellers attract their customers' attention. Which traders have the children noticed selling things in the street? Suggestions might include the ice cream van with its familiar tune; hot chestnuts or jacket potatoes for sale in the street. At the seaside children may have encountered candyfloss sellers and seafood stalls. Many children will probably have seen newspaper stalls and souvenir stalls at tourist sites. How are customers attracted to buy these goods?

Development
Using the background information explain that there were more street traders in the past. There were fewer shops and people sold things which they had made or grown themselves. Tell the children some of the cries they would use to sell their goods. Sing some of the familiar nursery rhymes which relate to street trading. For example, 'Simple Simon met a pieman going to the fair'; 'Have you seen the muffin man?' (The muffin man was quite a familiar sight, carrying a tray of muffins on his head and alerting potential customers by ringing a handbell as he walked along the streets.)

At Easter time, the hot cross buns seller would call in the streets, 'Hot cross buns, hot cross buns'. Talk about the different services which people would try to sell in the street. Call out some of the cries mentioned in the background information and ask the children to devise some more of their own.

Conclusion
Hand out the photocopiable sheet. Ask the children to complete the features and clothing of the street trader. Add the goods which the trader is selling in the basket.

Suggestion(s) for extension
Working in small groups ask the children to think of goods to sell or services to offer and encourage them to make up appropriate street cries and rhymes. When the children have practised their cries they can record them on tape. Play the tape back so that all the children are able to hear the different street cries.

Suggestion(s) for support
Some children might need help cutting out their completed street trader.

Assessment opportunities
Do children recognise the importance of street cries for catching buyers' attention? Can they talk about how street cries (and also songs and nursery rhymes) can be used as a source of information about shopping in the past?

Opportunities for IT
Children could use a word processor to write their street cries. If children are able to originate their work at the word processor this would encourage them to draft and redraft, using the editing facilities. They may need to be shown how to move the cursor around their text, to delete and edit their work without erasing too much that they have typed. If the cry is short they may want to retype each new version

underneath the last, or copy certain sections of it into the new version. In this way they could go back to a previous version and rework it. They might also need to save and reload their work to continue it at a later date. This could be done in pairs or small groups.

Finally children could decide how they were going to present their street cry, possibly using different sized fonts, centring or using bold or italic text. Each group could print out their final street cry, add pictures, either drawn by hand or with an art package and the full set could be bound into a class book.

If the children have access to a talking word processor, where words that are typed at the keyboard can be spoken back, they can listen to their street cries as they work on them. Alternatively if the school has access to a microphone that can be connected to the computer so that the sounds can be recorded and stored onto a disc the children could even recite their street cries and have the computer play them back to them in their own voices.

Display ideas
Create a background that depicts a street scene from a period long ago. Cut out the street traders which the children have completed from the photocopiable sheet and stick them on to the street scene. Ask each child to add a speech bubble beside their traders and then write the words of the street cry inside.

Reference to photocopiable sheet
The photocopiable sheet on page 129 shows an outline of a street trader carrying a basket. The children can complete the street trader, by adding clothes and facial features. Goods which were being sold can be drawn in the basket.

SHOP SIGNS

To learn about shops and shopping in the past and to draw comparisons with today.

†† *Whole class; individuals.*

🕐 *Whole class 20 minutes; individuals 30 minutes.*

Previous skills/knowledge needed
This activity will draw on children's awareness of buying and selling and how goods arrive in the shops.

Key background information
Before industrialisation most goods which were sold in shops were made on the same premises. Children were apprenticed to master craftsmen or traders in order to learn particular skills. Their family paid a sum of money to a master and the apprentice then went to live with his master's family. After several years of training, the apprentices then became masters themselves and were permitted to join a guild. The guilds existed to look after their members and they ensured that standards were maintained.

Similar trades were often located close together, for example in York, the butchers had their shops in the shambles. Other street names provide evidence of earlier trades for example Bread Lane, Fish Hill, Weavers' Row. Shops opened out directly onto the street. Inside there was a large counter with a workshop behind. The shop front had no glass windows and shutters were put up only during bad weather or at night.

Many surnames used today derive from former trades, for example, Smith, Cooper, Tailor, Cook, Baker, Butcher, Weaver, Carpenter, Fisher, Tanner, Mason, Miller, Tyler, Spicer, and Wright.

Preparation
Prepare enough of the photocopiable sheet on page 130 for each child. Cut out pieces of paper of suitable size to make large shop signs.

Resources needed

Collection of pictures/articles, bought in shops to talk about, for example shoes; clothes; gloves; bag; bread; fish and meat. Pencils, crayons, felt-tipped pens. Books and pictures of medieval and Tudor shops. Paper for large shop-sign designs. Photocopiable sheet on page 130.

What to do

Look at different articles included in the resources and talk with the children about where they came from. Where were they bought? Where were they made before arriving in the shop? Use the background information to explain that in the past most goods were made on the shop premises. Describe what the shops would look like. Look at the articles again and talk about which shops would have sold them in the past. Some children might be surprised that shops only sold one type of object and contrast this with current supermarkets and department stores selling many goods. Most people could not read so shopkeepers put a sign hanging outside their shop denoting what goods they were selling.

Hand out the photocopiable sheet and talk about the shops which the children can see on the paper. The signs above the shops have been left blank. Ask the children to draw suitable objects on the signs to denote what the shop is selling. Talk about other shops and ask the children to design a large shop sign on a piece of paper.

Suggestion(s) for extension

Encourage the children to make their own shops using reclaimed or construction materials. Can they make a counter and a shutter which will open and close the shop? Ask the children to investigate the origins of different surnames and the trades associated with them. Can they find out what a miller, a smith or a mason did?

Suggestion(s) for support

If necessary, limit the number of shops talked about. Use the photocopiable sheet as a reference tool and ask the children to draw a large sign for one of the shops on a big piece of paper.

Assessment opportunities

Can the children talk about differences between shopping now and in the past? They might suggest visits to many different shops, less choice, waiting for goods to be made.

Opportunities for IT

Children could use an art or drawing package to make their own shop signs and add text to their pictures. They would need to be introduced to the simple drawing tools, such as line drawing, changing the thickness of the line, making and re-sizing shapes such as circles and squares and adding colour to their work. They will also need to be shown how to add and position the text, selecting and sizing the fonts to fit the page that they have. This work is likely to take some time and children may need to save and retrieve their work so that they can continue at a later date.

Display ideas

Create a large wall display of a row of shops. Add the goods which they are selling and place the shop signs above them.

Reference to photocopiable sheet

The photocopiable sheet on page 130 shows a street scene, with shops opening out onto the street. The shops depicted are a bakers, a tailors and a butchers.

A VICTORIAN SCHOOLROOM

To identify differences between classrooms today and in a Victorian school room. To develop experience in interpreting how ways of life in the past can be represented.

†† *Whole class then pairs.*

🕐 *Whole class 15 minutes; pairs 20 minutes.*

Previous skills/knowledge needed

This activity will draw on children's knowledge about their own classrooms and experience of school.

Key background information

The 1870 Education Act led to the building of many new schools and the refurbishment of older ones. Windows were generally narrow and set up high so that it was difficult to see through them. Children sat at desks in long rows facing the front. Classrooms were often cold places, heated by a single stove in the corner of the room. Sometimes lessons were halted for children to do exercises to keep warm. Classrooms looked quite bare, with few pictures on the wall and little equipment. Children were expected to remain in their seats, listening carefully to the teacher or copying from the blackboard.

Preparation

Prepare the photocopiable sheet on page 131, per pair of children in your class.

Resources needed

Photocopiable sheet on page 131. Pencils. Photographs and books of school rooms in the past.

What to do

Introduction

Discuss with the children the classroom you are using. Ask the children to describe its different features. Can the children identify the classroom's most important features and give reasons for some of their comments? With the children make a list of things which a modern classroom needs.

Development

Ask the children if they think classrooms have always been like their present one. Can they think of any differences? Tell the children that they are going to look at a picture of a classroom from about a hundred years ago. An artist has collected a lot of information about the different features of this classroom and has drawn a picture of what the classroom might have looked like. Hand out one photocopiable sheet to share between pairs of children. Ask the children to be responsible for one half of the picture and to circle all the differences they can see between their present classroom and the Victorian classroom.

Conclusion

When the children have completed the activity they have to explain to their partner why they have circled particular features. Ask the children to discuss their findings in different groups or as a whole class discussion. Children will be able to compare these findings with other sources of information if there are other books and pictures about Victorian classrooms available.

Suggestion(s) for extension

Children can write down all the differences which they have noted on separate pieces of paper. They can then try and arrange the papers to prioritise the most important differences. Talk about the difference between the scene on the photocopiable sheet and the photographs used in books as sources of evidence. The photocopiable sheet is secondary evidence, as the artist has looked at photographs of Victorian classrooms (primary evidence) and has used them to recreate an impression of what a Victorian schoolroom would have looked like.

Suggestion(s) for support

Pair children of different abilities to support each other during this activity. Alternatively use the photocopiable sheet to promote group or whole class discussion.

A Victorian school room

Assessment opportunities

Can the children talk about some of the differences between the classrooms? Listen to whether the children can describe what it might have been like working in the Victorian school. Do the children recognise the different sources of evidence which can be used to find information about the past?

Display ideas

Use the pictures of Victorian school rooms as sources of information to recreate your own Victorian School in the classroom. Re-arrange the classroom furniture or use a separate play area and re-enact some Victorian lessons. Ask the children to research what items to include and encourage them to make some replicas if appropriate. Include a variety of different writing and reading materials and a blackboard. Costumes for the Victorian children could include pinafores for the girls and shirts and waistcoats for the boys. Include a long skirt for the teacher to wear. A stove could be made from cardboard boxes and a coal scuttle filled with crumpled up paper.

Reference to the photocopiable sheet

The photocopiable sheet on page 131 shows a reconstruction of a Victorian schoolroom. Features of this are: windows are high up on the wall; stove at the front; desks in rows; teachers desk at the front; large framed abacus; large portrait of Queen Victoria; the Union Jack; gas lights; blackboard; inkpots and pens; sandtrays; teacher and children in appropriate dress; dunce's hat and thin cane.

BUILDING DIFFERENT BRIDGES

To recognise changing designs in bridge building and to draw some conclusions about ways of life in the past using bridges as evidence. To sequence the bridges in chronological order.

†† *Whole class; groups; individuals/pairs.*

🕒 *Whole class 10 minutes; groups 20 minutes; individuals/pairs 20 minutes.*

Previous skills/knowledge needed

This activity will draw on children's current knowledge of different bridges in the environment.

Key background information

Finding ways of crossing rivers has been important from the earliest times. Many towns and cities developed as settlements because they provided a place where the river could be crossed either by bridge or a ford, for example, Bristol, London, Oxford. The pictures on the photocopiable

sheet show early ways of crossing rivers using stepping stones or fallen tree trunks. The medieval stone bridge has cutwaters to prevent the stonework from being worn away. People stood in the refuges to keep out of the way of horses and carts as they crossed the bridge. The arch gave bridges added strength. The first bridge in England to be made of iron was built in 1779 in Shropshire at a place which subsequently became known as Ironbridge. The Clifton Suspension bridge in Bristol was designed by Isambard Kingdom Brunel and built between 1832-1864. The Forth railway bridge is a cantilever bridge constructed out of steel tubes. It spans the Firth of Forth and is 2528 metres long. It was built between 1882 and 1890.

Preparation

If possible make a visit to any bridges in your locality to provide points of reference back in the classroom. Prepare enough strips of card for the timeline for each child/pairs of children. Photocopy sufficient numbers of the sheet on page 132.

Resources needed

Collection of photographs/pictures and books of different bridges. Photocopiable sheet on page 132. Timeline strips, scissors and adhesive.

What to do

Introduction

Begin by discussing bridges in the locality with the children. Why have they been built? Talk about their shapes and the materials they are made of. Look at pictures of other bridges from your resources and ask the children to describe them.

Development

Tell the children that they are going to look at different bridges built in the past. Where would people need to have built bridges? What alternatives were there? Hand out the photocopiable sheets and ask the children in groups to describe the different bridges. Ask them to consider why they were built and who might have used them. What materials were used to construct them? Talk about the shape of the bridges. Which bridges were the strongest? Ask the children to identify the oldest type of bridge and listen carefully to their reasons. The children might suggest that stepping stones and fallen trees are ways which are still possible today. What do the bridges tell us about life at the time they were built? For example was there a lot of traffic? What sort of vehicles used the bridges? What sort of technology was available to people at the time?

Conclusion

Ask the children to cut out the pictures from the photocopiable sheet and to sort and group them. They might choose to do this in a variety of ways perhaps by age; materials used; shape; different purposes. Discuss the different ways the children have chosen and provide opportunities for them to explain what they have done. Ask the children to sequence the bridges in a timeline to show the changing design of bridges. They can then stick the pictures onto a strip of card and label them.

Suggestion(s) for extension

Children can write short descriptions and present information about the bridges beneath the pictures on their timeline. Writing what the bridges were made of and who used them for example. Encourage children to research other bridges to add to their timeline.

Suggestion(s) for support

Some children may have difficulty determining a date order since all the bridges could be in use today. Encourage these children to look for other clues in the pictures to help them decide on the chronological ordering. Limit the number of pictures for these children to sort and sequence. Children can add some of their own pictures and group the pictures into 'bridges built in the past' and 'bridges built now'.

Assessment opportunities

Can children discuss the features of the bridges to draw some conclusions about different ways of life in the past? Listen carefully to how the children talk about their sequence. What sort of reasons do they give to describe their order?

Different bridges

▲ Talk about these different bridges.

▲ What materials are they made from?

Listen to how the children talk about the pictures. What vocabulary and phrases do they use? How many ways are they able to sort the pictures?

Opportunities for IT

Children could use a CD-ROM to look for information on different types of bridges. The questions could be set up in advance by the teacher so that children have a clear purpose for their initial use. Older or more able children could be more independent with their use, creating searches on keywords or browsing the different sections of the CD-ROM looking for information.

Children could use a word processor to write a simple description of the bridges on a class timeline of bridges. They might also use information taken from the CD-ROM to help them. The children can decide how to present their word processed information.

Display ideas

Provide pictures of different bridges for children to look at and to copy the different designs in their own models, using reclaimed or construction materials. Encourage the children to test the strengths of different bridges.

Reference to photocopiable sheet

The photocopiable sheet on page 132 shows stepping stones; a tree trunk lying across a river; a medieval stone bridge; Ironbridge; Clifton Suspension bridge, Bristol; the Forth Railway bridge, a modern bridge spanning a motorway and a pedestrian footbridge crossing a dual carriageway road.

We looked at different bridges

This aqueduct was built by the Romans. It carried water

This was the first iron bridge

The new road bridge to the Isle of Skye. This bridge has just been opened.

Sarah made this tree trunk bridge using an old _____ then roll

Kevin made this bridge using thin card and cereal boxes

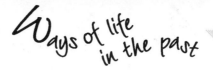
GROWING CORN; THE FARMER'S YEAR

To learn about the harvest cycle and compare farming in the past with methods used today. To explore the effects of mechanisation on everyday life.

†† *Whole class; individual.*

🕐 *Whole class 20 minutes; individual 20 minutes.*

Previous skills/knowledge needed

Some experience of planting seeds and watching plants grow would be helpful.

Key background information

The pictures on the photocopiable sheet show farming in medieval times. Similar methods of farming were employed both before and after this period. In the autumn or spring the land would be ploughed using oxen to pull the plough. The seed was sown by sowers walking along the furrows scattering the seed as they walked. Children were often employed to scare the birds away by shouting or firing stones with a sling. Scaring birds was common amongst children throughout the ages until compulsory schooling began in the latter part of the nineteenth century. The corn was cut with a scythe or sickle and bound into sheaves to dry in the sun. Once dry, the sheaves were taken into the threshing barn where the corn was separated from the straw with a flail. The corn was gathered into sacks to be taken to the flour mill. Some seed was left for planting the next year's crops. All the grains of corn were valuable and gleaners went into the fields to gather up the leftover grains. This activity can be followed up in the 'Making Flour' activity on page 41.

Preparation

Prepare the photocopiable sheet on page 133, one per child.

Resources needed

Books and pictures of modern and old farming methods. Stalks/seeds of corn. Photocopiable sheet 133. Pencils and colouring materials.

What to do

Introduction

Look at some stalks of corn with the children. Have they seen corn growing? Do they know how it is grown? Familiarise the children with the sequence of farming jobs which occur throughout the year such as, ploughing, planting and harvesting corn, referring to books and pictures if available.

Development

Hand out the photocopiable sheet and ask the children to identify what is happening in the modern farming pictures. Look at the pictures of the more traditional farming methods on the sheet. Can the children suggest what is happening

and compare with what happens now? Encourage the children to note some of the major differences for example, lack of machinery – everything was done by hand; no tractors to pull the ploughs. There are some similarities too notably the shape of the furrows. Talk about the different jobs which the children would be expected to help with. Explain that in the past they would all have been involved in the harvest, and had longer summer holidays so that they could be out in the field. Emphasise the importance of the harvest in providing people with enough to eat throughout the year. A good harvest was a time for celebration.

Conclusion

The sheet can be used in several ways. Children can draw lines to match old farming methods with their modern equivalents. Alternatively the children can cut out the pictures and sequence the pictures to tell a traditional and modern harvest story.

Suggestion(s) for extension

Children might like to make their own book of the harvest sequence. They can write about the different stages and use the pictures from the photocopiable sheet as well as their own drawings to illustrate their book. Alternatively they can make a 'then and now' farming book and contrast different farming methods.

Suggestion(s) for support

The farming sequence can be reinforced through traditional stories such as *The Little Red Hen*. The traditional farming sequence provides opportunities for children to role-play the different stages of ploughing, sowing, harvesting and threshing wheat.

Assessment opportunities

Can the children sequence the events in the correct order? Can the children talk about differences between traditional and modern farming methods and suggest how people's lives might have been affected? They might include the importance of a good harvest to have enough to eat; length of time it took to plough a field; everybody working on the land.

Harvest

Display ideas

Many paintings depict harvest scenes. Try and incorporate some within a display to help children appreciate how harvest has been represented in the past. Suitable pictures might include; *July* from *Les Très Riches Heures du Duc de Berry* by the Limbourg brothers c1415, *The Harvesters* by Pieter Bruegel the Elder, 1565, *Reapers* by George Stubbs, 1784.

Reference to photocopiable sheet

The photocopiable sheet on page 133 shows oxen ploughing the soil; a sower sowing seed 'broadcast' and cutting the corn by hand with a sickle. Modern equivalents which are illustrated include a tractor pulling a plough; a tractor pulling a seed-drill and a combine harvester. The pictures can be matched (old with new) and placed in order.

FIRE FIGHTING

To learn about the changing design of fire-fighting equipment. Use this knowledge to sequence fire-fighting equipment chronologically.

†† *Whole class; pairs; whole class; pairs/individuals.*

🕐 *Whole class 20 minutes; pairs 15 minutes; whole class 10 minutes; pairs/individuals 20 minutes.*

Previous skills/knowledge needed

This activity will draw on children's current knowledge of the fire service.

Key background information

Fire was an ever present danger in towns and villages where houses were built of timber and thatch. Open fires used for cooking and candles meant there was always the possibility of sparks setting houses alight. The most frequently used method to extinguish fires involved chains of people handing buckets of water to each other. Following the Great Fire of London (1666) several different sorts of pumps began to be used; water was pumped into hoses which could then be directed to the main area of the blaze.

A steam pump was invented in 1829 which used steam from a boiler to pump water to heights of ninety feet. These pumps gradually replaced the manual pumps. It took about ten minutes for them to build up sufficient steam as the fire engines rushed to the fire. Fire engines didn't use bells until 1903 and the 'hi-hi' man would sit at the front of the engine, or the whole crew would shout 'hi-ya-hi', to clear the streets. Before telephones were widespread, street fire alarms would be pressed to alert the fire brigade. Ordinary ladders were used to help people escape from buildings. In 1836 The Royal Society for the Protection of Life from Fire paid for extending ladders on wheels which could be rushed to scenes of fire. Fire services were organised by local communities to meet their needs and today the fire service is still in the control of local authorities.

Preparation

Prepare strips of card on which the children can stick their fire fighting sequence. Photocopiable sheet on page 134, enough for one per child.

Resources needed

Pictures of the modern fire service. Adhesive, scissors. Strip of card for the timeline. Photocopiable sheet on page 134.

What to do

Introduction

Begin by talking with the children about the procedure for raising the alarm and calling out the fire service. Discuss the fire service's response to a 999 call and how fire engines rush to the scene with their sirens blaring and lights flashing.

Look at the uniform which the firefighters wear and the equipment which they use to extinguish fires.

Development

Ask the children for their views on what it might have been like in the past. Do they think firefighters used the same equipment/wore the same clothes? Ask the children to form a human chain, passing a bucket along to each other to reach the end of the line. Did it take a very long time for the bucket to reach its destination?

Talk about hoses and the water being pumped through the hoses. Ask the children if they think this would be more effective than the human chain as a method of putting out fires. Talk about sources of water for the hoses and discuss fire hydrants in the street. Have children seen any of them?

Hand out the photocopiable sheet and ask the children to look at the different pictures. Working with a partner the children can each choose one picture and describe it. What things look the same and what things look different? Can the children explain any reasons for the differences? Children can report back to the rest of the class on some of their observations.

Conclusion

Ask the children to cut out the pictures and arrange them in a sequence beginning with the oldest. Encourage them to discuss the reasons for the way in which they have sequenced their pictures. They can then stick the pictures onto a strip of card to create a fire fighting timeline.

Suggestion(s) for extension

Children can write about the different fire fighting engines and equipment beneath their pictures. Encourage the children to find out more about the history of fire fighting.

Suggestion(s) for support

Children who have difficulty arranging all the pictures can simply sort pictures into sets of 'now' and 'then'. Encourage these children to look for similarities and differences without having to place the pictures in a chronological order. Some children might like to try making their own water pumps and hoses using equipment in the water tray.

▲ Cut out the pictures and make a timeline.

Fire fighting

Assessment opportunities

Can the children recognise the fire engines of the past? Can the children sequence the pictures correctly? Can they identify similarities and differences and suggest reasons for their observations?

Reference to photocopiable sheet

The photocopiable page 134 shows the changing designs of fire engines. The pictures are of a hand operated pump used in the seventeenth century, a Victorian horse-drawn fire engine, a 1930s fire engine and a modern fire engine.

MOTORING IN THE PAST

To learn about motoring at the turn of the century, from different sources.
†† *Whole class; individual.*
🕐 *Whole class 25 minutes; individual 25 minutes.*

Previous skills/knowledge needed

Children will need to draw on their knowledge of cars and motoring today.

Key background information

The first successful petrol driven car was made in Germany in the 1880s. At this time cars were expensive and not very reliable. The shapes of many early cars resembled those of carriages pulled by horses. Originally the tyres were made of solid rubber, but pneumatic tyres were developed in 1888. Some early cars had a tiller to steer with rather than a steering wheel. Few cars had roofs at first, but later, collapsing hoods which could be put up when it rained were added. Small windscreens provided some protection for the driver and passengers, and early windscreen wipers were operated by

keep them warm; goggles protected the driver from dust blowing up from the road.

Conclusion

Ask the children to connect the labels to the appropriate places on the photocopiable sheet by drawing arrows. Encourage children to draw a picture of a modern car and to label things which they would take on a car journey today, on another sheet of paper.

Suggestion(s) for extension

Pretend to be one of the passengers or the driver in the picture. Talk or write about what your car is like. Describe the clothes you are wearing and the things you are taking with you on your journey.

Suggestion(s) for support

Some children will need help reading the labels at the bottom of the photocopiable sheet. If they find difficulty with the cutting and gluing, limit the activity to talking about the picture.

Assessment opportunities

Can the children identify differences between past and present motoring? Can the children use the information from the picture to make more general comments about life at the time. For example dusty roads, few petrol stations.

Display ideas

Collect some of the objects mentioned on the photocopiable sheet and use them to create a display depicting motoring in the past. Provide opportunities for children to make comparisons by placing items taken on car journeys today beside them. Invite the children to bring in their own toy cars for the display and try to include some copies of older cars too. Equip the play area with some of the objects from the photocopiable sheet and re-organise the seating to provide opportunities for children to 'go motoring'.

hand. The headlights provided a dim light. Cars were started by turning a starting handle at the front of the car. Mudguards prevented dirt splashing up from the roads. Drivers wore goggles and women wore veils to keep the dust from their eyes. It was often very cold in the car; passengers carried thick rugs and foot muffs. Rubber covers could be attached to the car to cover up the passengers. Drivers carried their own tool chests and some spare parts since there were many breakdowns. Spare petrol was also carried since there were very few petrol stations.

Preparation

Before starting the activity ask the children to look carefully at their own family car or a car owned by a friend. Tell them to look at the size; shape; wheels; lights and windscreen. Prepare the photocopiable sheet on page 135 for each child.

Resources needed

Pictures and books of old cars. Scissors, paper, adhesive. Photocopiable sheet on page 135.

What to do

Introduction

Ask the children to describe their own or a friend's car. Discuss what it looks like and its different features. Show the children pictures of late Victorian and early twentieth century cars from your resources and ask the children to describe them. Can they recognise any significant differences, look at windscreens, lights, roofs, wheels and overall shape.

Development

Hand out the photocopiable sheet and talk about the picture. Ask the children to try and identify the different objects mentioned at the bottom of the sheet. Why would some of these objects be taken on the journey. What do they tell us about motoring in the past? For example, it was cold with no roof so people had rugs to

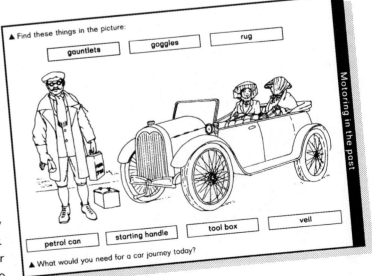

▲ Find these things in the picture:

gauntlets   goggles   rug

petrol can   starting handle   tool box   veil

Motoring in the past

▲ What would you need for a car journey today?

Reference to photocopiable sheet

The photocopiable sheet on page 135 shows an early twentieth century car with seated passengers and a driver standing beside it. Included in the picture are: collapsing hood; starting handle; tin of petrol; tool box. The driver is wearing goggles, a dust coat and gauntlets. The women passengers are wearing veils and are covered with a thick rug.

THE BICYCLE

To compare bicycles seen today with a Victorian penny farthing.

†† *Whole class; pairs; individual.*

🕐 *Whole class 20 minutes; pairs 5 minutes; individual 20 minutes.*

Previous skills/knowledge needed

Close observation/measuring skills.

Key background information

The earliest bicycle, the hobby horse, was designed at the beginning of the nineteenth century. It comprised two wheels, linked by a wooden beam which had a saddle mounted on the top. Riders sat on the saddle and moved along by pushing their feet against the ground. The first cycle to have pedals was built by a blacksmith, Kirkpatrick Macmillan in 1839, but his design never became popular. The penny farthing appeared in the 1870s with pedals to propel the bike along. They were difficult to mount and falls were common. Penny farthings had an iron frame and solid rubber tyres. The largest penny farthings had front wheels standing 210cm high. In 1885 the Rover Safety cycle, designed by J K Starley heralded the design of bicycles as we know them today. Within 10 years 800,000 had been built. The pneumatic tyre, developed by John Boyd Dunlop in 1888 also made cycling more comfortable.

Preparation

Before starting this activity ask the children to look carefully at their own bicycle (or a bicycle belonging to a friend or relation) and to be prepared to describe what it looks like. Prepare the photocopiable sheet on page 136 for each child.

Resources needed

Magazines and catalogues with pictures of different bikes, pictures of old and new bikes. Pencils and colouring materials. Photocopiable sheet (page 136). Measuring equipment.

What to do

Introduction

Begin by talking about modern bicycles. Encourage the children to describe them and how they work. What makes them move? What features and equipment do different bikes have? Refer to pictures of modern bikes from resources if they are available.

Development

Tell the children that they are going to learn about a bicycle which was made over a hundred years ago. Measure out 210 cm against the side of the classroom wall. This was the height of the front wheel of a penny farthing. Ask one child to stand beside this to gain an appreciation of scale. Hand out the photocopiable sheet of the penny farthing and ask the children to work in pairs and to note any differences between the penny farthing and modern bikes. Explain why the bikes were called penny farthings and talk about penny and farthing coins. Talk about how difficult it was to get on and to ride. Ask the children to draw a modern bike beneath the penny farthing, showing as many differences as they can think of.

Suggestion(s) for extension

Children can investigate other bicycles and then construct a bicycle timeline, for example the hobby horse; safety bicycles and tricycles.

Suggestion(s) for support

Children might prefer to find a picture from a magazine. Cut it out and stick it beneath the penny farthing.

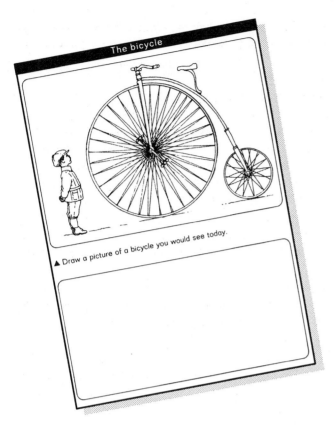

The bicycle

▲ Draw a picture of a bicycle you would see today.

Assessment opportunities

Can the children describe any differences and similarities between the penny farthing and the modern bicycle?

Opportunties for IT

Children could use an art or drawing package to draw simple outline or silhouette shapes of the different types of bikes. This would encourage them to experiment with drawing straight lines and making and re-sizing circles for the wheels. If the software has a 'snap to grid facility' this could be used so that when the children draw straight lines for the bicycle frame they are automatically adjusted so that they lock into a background grid of squares.

Each of the pictures could be printed out and used on a class timeline. Add word processed text giving details about the bike itself. With most modern word processors it is possible to use the picture drawn in an art package and place it onto the page. The text can be added at appropriate places.

Display ideas

Make a life-size model of a penny farthing. Draw around a child and cut out a life-size outline. Dress the cut-out figure in late Victorian clothes and stand it beside the penny farthing so that the children can develop an appreciation of the size of the wheel.

Reference to photocopiable sheet

The photocopiable sheet on page 136 shows a picture of a penny farthing. Space has been left beneath for children to draw or stick a picture of a modern bicycle.

SHIPBUILDING LONG AGO

To learn how William the Conqueror built his ships, by using the Bayeux tapestry as a source of information.
†† *Whole class; groups; individuals.*
🕐 *Whole class 25 minutes; groups 15 minutes; individuals 15 minutes.*

Previous skills/knowledge needed

This activity can be used in conjunction with the story of the battle of Hastings page 103.

Key background information

As well as recording the Battle of Hastings in 1066, the Bayeux tapestry also records events prior to the battle. Preparations for William the Conqueror's invasion of England are included which provide a great deal of information about life at the time.

The construction of William's ships followed traditional Viking designs. Wooden planks were joined with iron nails and caulking made from tarred wool was packed between the gaps to ensure that the ship was watertight. The ship was guided by a large paddle, which acted as a rudder. The bottom of the mast was held steady by a huge block of wood, known as the mastfish. Sails were used at sea, but the sailors also used oars to propel the ship into land. The prows of the ships were adorned with fierce animal heads which could be removed on the approach to land.

Preparation

Prepare the photocopiable sheet on page 137 for each child.

Resources

Pictures of Anglo-Saxon and Viking ships. Photocopiable sheet on page 137. Pencils, crayons and felt-tipped pens.

What to do

Introduction

Talk to the children about the different ships and boats they have seen. What sorts are they and what do they carry? Who travels on different ships and boats and for what reason? What makes the ships and boats move in the water? Talk about the different sources of power for example wind, steam, engine and oars.

HISTORY KS1

Development

Tell the children they are going to look at ships which were made about a thousand years ago. Look at the pictures of Anglo-Saxon and Viking ships from the resources and ask the children to describe them. What are they made of? What makes them move through the water? Did they move quickly? What were they used for? Would it be comfortable travelling in these ships?

Hand out the photocopiable sheets. Set the context of the pictures by explaining William the Conqueror's plans to invade England and his need to transport his army, together with their weapons, horses and provisions across the English Channel from Normandy. The pictures have been taken from scenes depicted on the Bayeux tapestry. Talk about what is happening in the different pictures and ask the children to describe how the ships are being made. Divide the class into four different groups and give each group a picture from the photocopiable sheet to work from. Ask the children to mime the part of the shipbuilding process which is illustrated in their picture. When the children have practised, the different groups can show their mimes to provide a sequence of the shipbuilding process.

Conclusion

Using books and pictures from your resources, ask the children to complete the final picture of the ship by adding a rudder, sail and fierce prow. They might also like to add some passengers.

Suggestion(s) for extension

Children might like to write about the different stages of shipbuilding shown on the sheet. Children could continue to practise their mimes and add sound effects to their shipbuilding sequence. Encourage the children to find out more about ships in the past. Investigate what they were made from and how they were made. What powered the ships? Who used them and for what purpose?

Suggestion(s) for support

Some children might find the final picture on the photocopiable sheet too small to complete. Provide them with a large sheet of paper and ask them to draw the completed boat, referring to illustrations and pictures.

Assessment opportunities

Can the children describe the shipbuilding process? Do they think that the Bayeux tapestry is a good source of information about ships in the past? What doesn't the tapestry tell us?

Opportunities for IT

Children might be able to use a CD-ROM to look for specific information about Viking or Norman ships.

Display ideas

Ask children to research different boats from the past and draw or model them to be placed on a classroom timeline.

Reference to photocopiable sheet

The photocopiable page 137 illustrates different stages in shipbuilding which are recorded in the Bayeux tapestry. The first four pictures show men cutting down trees with axes; planing the tree trunks into planks of wood; drilling holes and planing the ship's sides and finally, hammering the planks of wood together to make the ship. The fifth picture is a large outline of a ship for the children to complete.

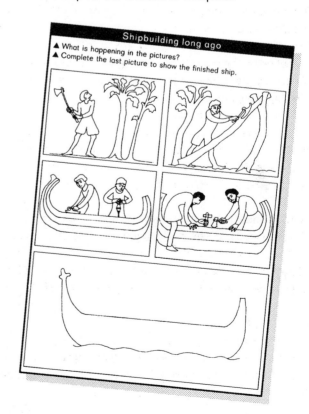

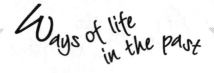

A CANAL BARGE

To learn about canals and investigate differences in the ways goods are transported now and ways in which they were transported in the past.

†† *Whole class; individual.*

🕐 *Whole class 25 minutes; individuals 20 minutes.*

Previous skills/knowledge needed

Some awareness of how goods are transported in Britain today would be helpful.

Key background information

Canal building was important in the latter half of the eighteenth century and the early nineteenth century. Travel by road was slow and often expensive so alternative modes of transport were devised. Canals were built by gangs of labourers, (navvies), who dug out the canal by hand and used the earth to make the canal banks. The canal was made waterproof by stamping a mixture of clay and water into the canal bed. Canal boats carried a variety of cargo: coal; china clay; pottery; wood; stone; iron ore; tin; wire and copper, agricultural produce and various groceries. By 1830 there were 4000 miles of canals in Britain which linked the major industrial towns together. Horses were used to pull the boats along, although later in the nineteenth century steam engines were used.

Preparation

A visit to a canal if there is one in the locality would be a good starting point for this activity. Prepare one copy of photocopiable sheet on page 138 for each child.

Resources needed

Books and pictures of canals. Water tray. Toy boat with string attached. Photocopiable sheet on page 138. Pencils, crayons and felt-tipped pens.

What to do

Introduction

Talk to the children about how goods today are transported by roads. Do they know what some of the lorries carry and their possible destinations? Make a list with the children of the different goods. Where do the goods come from and where are they being transported to? Consider for example: food to shops, vegetables to markets, bricks to building sites, cars from factories to showrooms. Have a discussion about other forms of transport.

Development

Look at the list of modern goods which are transported by road today and ask the children which goods might also need to have been transported in the past. Can they think of any other goods which would have been moved then? Explain to the children some of the difficulties of road travel in the past, and ask them if they can think of any solutions for transporting different goods.

Ask the children to place the toy boat in the water and to pull it along with the string. Explain how cargo used to be carried on boats pulled by horses along the canals. Canal boats could carry heavier loads than wagons, more quickly and more cheaply. Fragile cargo such as pottery was carried more safely on the canals. Use the background information to explain how the canals were built.

Conclusion

Hand out the photocopiable sheet and talk about the picture. Children can complete the picture by adding someone to steer the boat and another person leading the horse along the tow-path. Ask the children to write what cargo the boat was carrying.

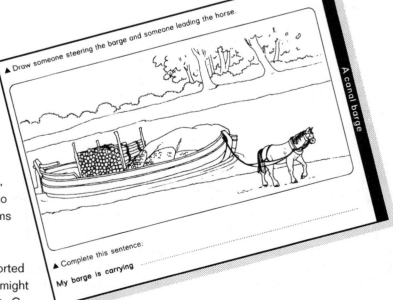

▲ Draw someone steering the barge and someone leading the horse.

A canal barge

▲ Complete this sentence:

My barge is carrying ....

Suggestion(s) for extension

Children can find out more information about ways of life on the canals. Encourage the children to investigate how the canals were constructed and how particular difficulties were overcome by building locks, tunnels and aqueducts.

Suggestion(s) for support

Children can talk about the cargo the boat is carrying. They might like to devise their own canal scene using the water tray with toy boats carrying different cargoes. A tow-path could be created beside the water tray and figures of people and horses could be used to pull the boats along with pieces of string.

Assessment opportunities

Can the children identify differences between how goods are transported now and how they were moved about the country in the past?

Reference to photocopiable sheet

The photocopiable page 138 shows a canal boat laden with cargo. Space has been left for the children to complete the picture and to write about the cargo the boat was carrying.

VEHICLES IN THE STREET 100 YEARS AGO

To learn about different vehicles seen in the street a hundred years ago and compare this with streets of today.

†† *Whole class; individual.*

🕐 *20 minutes whole class; 15 minutes individual.*

Key background information

Horse-drawn omnibuses were first used in the early nineteenth century to provide transport for those people who could not afford their own carriage. Their numbers steadily increased throughout the nineteenth century in conjunction with horse drawn trams which ran along rails laid in the road. Hansom cabs drawn by horses were the forerunners of modern taxis. The horses were guided by the driver standing at the back of the cab. Passengers gave the driver his instructions by opening a little hatch in the roof.

The first motor cars were built in the latter part of the nineteenth century and were only owned by the wealthy. Cars were restricted to travelling at 2mph in towns and 4mph on country roads and a man with a red flag was supposed to walk in front of them. In 1896, a Locomotives on Highways Act increased the speed limit to 14mph and scrapped the rule about the red flag. Many shops provided a delivery service for their better off customers. Depending on the sort of goods

to be delivered this could be a horse-drawn cart or a delivery boy on a bicycle.

Preparation

Prepare the photocopiable sheet on page 139, one per child.

Resources needed

Pictures and books about road transport now and 100 years ago. Photocopiable sheet on page139. Pencils and colouring materials.

What to do

Discuss with the children the variety and types of vehicles seen on roads today. Children could undertake a traffic survey of the type of vehicles passing their school, noting down cars, vans, bicycles, taxis, buses and lorries. Talk about the different purposes for travel, for example transporting goods, leisure and going to work. IT programs can be used to record this data.

Would people in the past have had the same reasons for travelling? What sort of vehicles would children 100 years ago have seen in the street? Refer to pictures showing different forms of road transport 100 years ago from your resources. Ask the children to describe the different vehicles. In what ways were they different from those of today? Hand out the photocopiable sheet and talk about the different vehicles. Compare the vehicles with those of today and identify similarities and differences. Ask the children to complete the sheet by drawing pictures of modern vehicles opposite their Victorian equivalents.

Suggestion(s) for extension

Children can investigate other forms of road transport. Ask them to draw pictures of other vehicles and use them to create a classroom timeline. Children might like to make their own book showing old and modern vehicles.

Suggestion(s) for support

Ask the children to identify one difference between Victorian and modern vehicles. Some children might find the spaces

Opportunities for IT

Children could record the results of their traffic survey using a simple graphing program. The class could decide in advance the different types of vehicles that they would count and then enter in the totals for each category. This could be used for drawing graphs of the different information.

Children could then use the bar charts produced to decide which was the most common vehicle type and why, or which was the least popular. Different groups could collect different types of information from the traffic count, colours of cars, numbers of passengers in a car, number of wheels on lorries or types of bikes. The resulting graph with their interpretation could be printed out and used as a class display.

Display ideas

Create a Victorian street scene to display the different forms of transport. Use paint and sponges to create the effect of paving stones. Ask the children to draw and paint different Victorian road vehicles which can then be placed on the street picture. Encourage the children to refer closely to books and pictures to ensure accurate representations of some of these vehicles.

Reference to photocopiable sheet

The pictures on the photocopiable sheet on page 139 depict a horse drawn bus; a hansom cab; a horse and cart delivering coal and a motor car.

on the photocopiable sheet too small to draw their pictures, so provide them with larger sheets of paper to draw their pictures on. Provide magazines for children to cut out pictures of different modern road vehicles to stick in their own road transport book. Ask the children to look in books to find pictures of old vehicles to compare with the pictures which they have cut out.

Assessment opportunities

Can the children identify differences between late nineteenth century and modern road vehicles. Can they use this knowledge to draw some conclusions about street life and conditions at the time. For example, the noise of the horses, smells, flies, safety?

A RAILWAY TIMELINE

To learn about different forms of rail transport and to use this knowledge to sequence a railway timeline in chronological order and note changes which have occurred in rail transport.

†† *Pairs. Whole class. Individuals/pairs.*

🕐 *Pairs 30 minutes. Whole class 15 minutes. Individuals/pairs 30 minutes.*

Previous skills/knowledge needed

Some vocabulary associated with the passage of time for example before, after, then, now.

Key background information

The earliest railways were used in the coal mines where horses were used for hauling heavy goods along iron rails. Engineers later developed steampower to haul the wagons. The first steam powered locomotive in Britain was designed by Richard Trevithick in 1801. Experiments with the design of steam powered locomotives continued to be developed in the mining industry. The first public railway to open was the Stockton to Darlington line in 1825. This railway carried both passengers and heavy goods. Stephenson designed

the Rocket locomotive to pull passengers and freight on the Liverpool and Manchester railway which opened in 1830.

New railway lines were rapidly constructed in the following years and by 1850 there were more than 6000 miles of railway tracks. The railways provided a quick, efficient and relatively cheap form of transport. Steam engines continued to be developed. The Mallard holds the world record for the fastest steam locomotive, travelling at 126mph. Diesel engines gradually replaced steam engines in the 1950s and 1960s.

Preparation
Prepare strips of card/paper for the timeline. Prepare the photocopiable sheet on page 140, one per child.

Resources needed
Pictures and books of different railways and trains. Strips of card/paper for the timeline. Scissors and adhesive. Photocopiable sheet on page 140. Pencils, a variety of crayons and felt-tipped pens.

What to do
Introduction
Begin by talking about railways. Have any of the children ever been on a train? Discuss the stages of a railway journey, for example buying a ticket; waiting at the station and choosing a carriage. Talk about specific features to note on a railway journey for example, rail track, signals, level crossings, tunnels and the people who work on the railway.
Development
Tell the children that they are going to look at different pictures of railways in the past. Hand out the photocopiable sheet and ask the children to work in pairs and to discuss the

different trains and railways which they can see. Encourage the children to look for similarities and differences between the different trains. How were the locomotives powered? Use the background information to provide additional information for the children and any pictures from your resources if available.
Conclusion
Ask the children to cut out the pictures from the photocopiable sheet and arrange them in chronological order beginning with the oldest train. Ask the children to give reasons for their order. How old do they think the trains are? Check the children's sequence and ask them to glue the pictures on to a strip of card to make their own railway timeline.

Suggestion(s) for extension
Children can write beneath the pictures a description of the different trains. Encourage the children to find out more information about the different trains to add to their timeline. Find out about the Stephensons and how they built their early engines. Use Victorian paintings as a source of information about rail travel in the nineteenth century, for example pictures by Abraham Solomon, William Powell Frith.

Suggestion(s) for support
If necessary reduce the number of pictures for the children to sequence. Ask the children to select a picture from the photocopiable sheet which shows a train today and another which shows a train in the past. Can they find any differences between the two trains? Children might like to build their own railway using trains and tracks available in the classroom.

Assessment opportunities

Can the children put the pictures in the correct chronological sequence and can they provide reasons for their sequence?

Opportunities for IT

If the school has a *Roamer* or *Pipp*, children could pretend it's a train. Mark out a simple train track on paper on the floor with a station, set of signals and a buffer. The children could be given different tasks to make *Roamer* go once around the track and stop at the station for a certain time and then go around again; or stop at the signals and then go up a siding and stop at the buffers. Children could try out

A railway timeline
▲ Cut out the pictures.

▲ Put the pictures in order, beginning with the oldest railway engine.

their commands on a model train made from play materials in the classroom.

This activity would introduce children to some of the control aspects of the National Curriculum such as giving sequences of commands to control movement. It will also involve children in estimating and preparing a logical sequence of commands. Children could record their key presses on a special sheet so that other groups could come and try out their solution to the problem.

Display ideas

Ask the children to design and build their own railway engine and bridge from reclaimed materials. Consider how the engine is going to be powered and what it is going to be used for (freight or passengers). Paint a backcloth of a railway station against which the models can be displayed.

Reference to photocopiable sheet

The photocopiable sheet on page 140 shows horses pulling the coal wagons; an early steam train on the Liverpool and Manchester Railway; a steam train at the beginning of this century; the 1930s Mallard; a 1960s diesel train; a modern high speed train.

VISITING A VICTORIAN SEASIDE RESORT

To learn about amusements at a Victorian seaside resort. To use evidence from a Victorian postcard scene to describe a Victorian holiday.

👫 *Whole class; individuals.*

🕐 *Whole class 15 minutes; individuals 50 minutes.*

Previous skills/knowledge needed

Knowledge of the seaside from different books and stories, and/or personal experience. This activity can be linked with 'Packing a Victorian suitcase' page 76.

Key background information

One of the most noticeable differences between beach scenes now and in the past is people's clothing. Only in the past thirty years have people begun to remove most of their clothes when they are on the beach! Bathing huts were a common feature in Victorian times. People changed in the huts which were then wheeled into the sea, bathers emerged from the doors at the front and plunged straight into the sea. Following their bathe, people would return to the hut which was then pulled back out of the sea. Many Victorian resorts built piers which provided amusements and entertainment for visitors. Punch and Judy shows and donkey rides were popular with young children.

Preparation

Find books with Victorian seaside scenes in and ask the children to bring in some postcards they have received at home, from holiday resorts. Prepare the photocopiable sheet on page 141, one per child.

Resources

The collection of holiday postcards. Pictures from travel brochures of holiday resorts. Books, pictures and photographs of Victorian seaside scenes. Pencils, crayons and felt-tipped pens. Photocopiable sheet on page 141.

What to do

Introduction

Talk to the children about going on holidays or trips. Where have they been? How did they travel to their destination? What sort of activities do they like to do on holiday? Did they eat any special foods? You might refer to some holiday brochures or postcards from the resource collection.

Development

Introduce the idea that they are going to find out about how people enjoyed themselves in the past. Do the children think that families enjoyed doing the same things a hundred years ago as they do today? If available, look at pictures and photographs of Victorian seaside scenes and ask the children to describe what they can see. Hand out the photocopiable sheet and talk about the scene shown. Identify the similarities and differences between a Victorian and modern beach scene. What sort of activities would the children enjoy doing?

Conclusion

Ask the children to imagine that they are on holiday a hundred years ago and to write a message on the second half of the photocopiable sheet as though it were their postcard home describing their holiday. Children can then colour the picture postcard.

At the seaside

▲ Write about your holiday at the seaside.

Suggestion(s) for extension

Encourage the children to try and find out more about how Victorian children amused themselves using different sources of information.

Suggestion(s) for support

This activity can be limited to a discussion of the Victorian beach scene, and children colouring the postcard. Children could identify which activities on the postcard they would like to engage in.

Assessment opportunities

Listen to some of the differences which the children note in the Victorian beach scene. Do the children use the information from the postcard scene in their message.

Display ideas

Create a large display of contrasting beach scenes, one set in Victorian times and a modern beach. Provide a background of sea and sand. Ask the children to draw and cut out people and objects to stick onto the different beach scenes.

Reference to photocopiable sheet

Photocopiable sheet on page 141 shows the front of a picture postcard of a Victorian beach scene. It includes a pier; children watching a Punch and Judy show and riding on donkeys; bathing huts on the beach and in the water; a family having a picnic. The second half of the sheet represents the reverse of the picture postcard and has been left blank for the children to fill in their message.

PACKING A VICTORIAN SUITCASE

To gain information about going on holiday in Victorian times using information gained from looking at artefacts. To use this information to compare the past with their own experiences and to draw some conclusions about life in Victorian times.

†† *Whole class and individuals.*

🕐 *Whole class 20 minutes; individuals 20 minutes.*

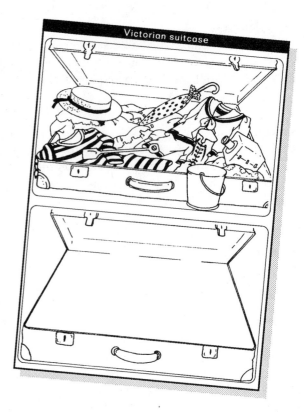

Victorian suitcase

Previous skills/knowledge needed

Knowledge of the seaside from different books and stories and/or personal experience.

Key background information

From the mid nineteenth century there was a tremendous expansion of the British seaside resorts. The seaside holiday and trips to the seaside were facilitated by the growth of the railway network which enabled people to travel to these resorts more easily. Stopping work for a few days' holiday became more common and day trips and outings were enjoyed by many more people.

Preparation

Collection of resources for a display of objects which might be taken on holiday or a trip today. Choose a selection, for example sun cream; camera; swimming costumes; bucket and spade; fishing net; sun hat; sunglasses; beach ball; armbands or swimming rings. Prepare the photocopiable sheet on page 142, one per child.

Resources needed

Seaside display objects. Pictures and books showing aspects of Victorian life. Photocopiable sheet on page 142. Pencils, crayons and felt-tipped pens.

What to do

Introduction

Talk about going on trips and holidays. Where have the children been? What things did they pack to take with them? Why did they need these things? Use the resources mentioned above to stimulate the discussion.

Development

Ask the children if they think children living a 100 years ago would have taken the same things. Hand out the photocopiable sheet and identify things which are the same and those which are different. Ask the children to describe how some of the objects are different, for example, the swimming costume has long legs and sleeves. What do the contents of the suitcase tell you about how Victorian children enjoyed themselves at the seaside? Can the children suggest some of the activities the Victorian children are going to do? If available from the resources, you might refer to other pictures showing Victorian seaside scenes. The contents of the suitcase would have belonged to wealthier Victorian children. Point out that many children would not have had all these possessions.

Conclusion

Ask the children to draw things they would take on a holiday now in the suitcase provided on the photocopiable sheet.

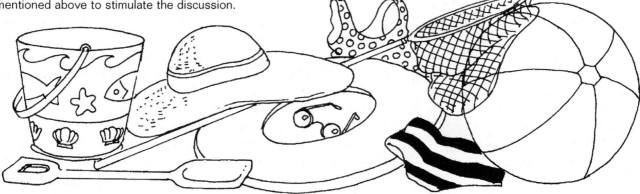

Suggestion(s) for extension

Children can write about some of the objects in the suitcase and explain why they were taken and their modern equivalent. They might like to write a story set in the past which included children using or playing with some of these objects. Encourage children to research other objects which a Victorian family might take on holiday.

Suggestion(s) for support

Some children might need help identifying the differences. Pictures of modern seaside scenes might be useful for them to refer to when they are drawing their suitcase contents.

Assessment opportunities

Can the children identify similarities and differences between ways of life in Victorian times and now? Do they use the articles in the suitcase as evidence to support their observations about life in the past? For example, noticing 'it would have taken a long time to do up your boots in the morning with all those buttons'.

Opportunities for IT

Children could use a word processor to write a packing list for their Victorian suitcase. They could also write a similar list for a modern suitcase and present the two side by side.

If the children use a simple desktop publishing package, or can set their word processor for two columns the two lists can appear together on a single page. The modern day equivalents of the Victorian articles could be added in the second column.

Display ideas

The collection of objects to be taken on trips today can be displayed alongside pictures showing things taken in Victorian times. Children might also like to draw some pictures of different Victorian objects, using pictures from books as different sources of information.

Reference to photocopiable sheet

The photocopiable sheet on page 142 shows an open suitcase with the following articles resembling the contents of a Victorian suitcase: an old camera; old bathing trunks/ swimming costumes; parasol; boater; button-up boots; a tin bucket and a wooden spade; frilly dress and petticoat; sailor outfit for a boy. The second half of the sheet provides an 'empty suitcase' for the children to 'pack'.

PLAYGROUND GAMES

To gain information about children's games and to recognise similarities and differences between games played now and in the past.

†† *Whole class then individual.*

⏱ *Whole class 20 minutes; individual 30 minutes.*

Previous skills/knowledge needed

This will draw on children's knowledge of playground games which they play now and any information they may have of traditional playground games.

Key background information

This activity will enable children to draw comparisons between playground games now and in the past. It provides an opportunity for the children to develop awareness of continuity and that the present has many links with the past.

Preparation

Take some photographs of children at school playing different games in the playground. Prepare 'then and now' folders by folding a large sheet of paper in half. Prepare the photocopiable sheet on page 143 per pair of children.

Resources needed

Photographs of playground games. Photocopiable sheet on page 143. 'Then and now' folders. Pencils, crayons and felt-tipped pens. Books and pictures of children playing in the past. Cassette player.

What to do

Introduction

Begin by looking at the photographs taken of children playing games in the playground today. What games are they playing and how do they play them? Ask the children to explain the rules. Who plays these games? Who teaches them how to play these games and how did they learn them?

Development

Explain to the children that they are going to investigate games which were played about 100 years ago. Hand out the photocopiable sheet and talk about the different games which the children can see. Do children still play these games

Ways of life in the past

today? Ask the children if they can think of any other games which children might have played in the past. Refer to additional information from books and pictures if available.

Conclusion
Hand out the 'then and now' folders. Ask the children to draw and colour pictures of children playing games on the different sides of the folder. They can label the different games which they have drawn.

Suggestion(s) for extension
Children can make small books of instructions for the games which they play now for people to read in the future. Children might like to write or record some of the songs and rhymes which they sing and say in the playground.

Children can ask their parents and other adults about the games which they played and the songs and rhymes they sang in the playground. Are they similar to the rhymes they know? They can compare their findings with their knowledge of the present day playground and what they have learned about playgrounds 100 years ago.

Suggestion(s) for support
Some children will need help labelling the different games which they have drawn.

Assessment opportunities
Do the children recognise that not everything has changed from the past? Can they recognise similarities with games played today?

Opportunities for IT
The class could make a booklet of instructions for playground games, now or in the past using the word processor. Children could work in small groups to write the instructions, save them to disc, print them out and give them to another group

to try out to make sure they work. They could then come back to the computer and edit or amend their original text and try again. Children can decide on the fonts and format for the final version before it is printed. Pictures could be added, either drawn on by hand or taken from clip art, or they may be drawn by the children using a suitable art or drawing package.

An alternative activity could be to make a collection of playground rhymes past and present. These could be typed into the word processor and formatted by the children into an interesting display, with pictures added. The completed collection could be printed and bound and then displayed in the class or school library.

Display ideas
Create a large display showing different playground games. A school window could provide a frame. This would create the impression that one is inside the school, looking through the window to the playground outside. The small books the children have written to provide instructions for the different games could be placed at the front of the display along with any other resources or reference materials used. Encourage the children to record some of their playground games and rhymes and leave the tape available for them to listen to or add to.

Reference to the photocopiable sheet
The photocopiable sheet on page 143 shows children playing different games in a Victorian playground. The games include: marbles; spinning tops; boys kicking an old tin can; hopscotch; skipping; leapfrog; hoops.

▲ Can you find children playing these games in the picture?

rolling hoops   hopscotch   spinning tops   leap frog

marbles   tin-can-football   skipping

78

HISTORY KS1

Famous men and women

This section provides information and activities linked to the lives of famous men and women in the past. The selection of people has taken into account the requirements of the History Areas of Study at Key Stage 1 and includes personalities from different periods of time. Personalities from different sections of society, who have been remembered for many different reasons have also been included. For example, rulers, saints, engineers, pioneers and inventors, together with particular well known personalities. Children are encouraged to investigate some of the sources of information which tell us about particular personalities. Some activities encourage children to investigate how the stories of certain famous people have developed. Children are also encouraged to reflect whether certain personalities were important and should still be remembered.

The stories of many of these personalities provide opportunities for children to sequence events and to explain the order of their sequences. The activities provide opportunities for children to explore why people did things and the results of their actions. Many of the stories also provide background information about ways of life in the past and the attitudes and values held by people in the past. The activities are designed to encourage children to communicate their awareness and understanding of the past in different ways. They include writing accounts, drawings and paintings, model making and role-play activities.

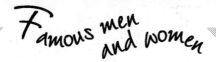
GUY FAWKES

To learn about Guy Fawkes and the Gunpowder Plot through songs and firework celebrations. To sequence the main events of the story in chronological order.

†† *Whole class/individual.*

🕐 *Whole class 20 minutes; individual variable.*

Previous skills/knowledge needed
Children will draw on their story-writing skills.

Key background information
The Gunpowder Plot was hatched by Guy Fawkes and a group of his friends in 1605 to kill King James I. Guy Fawkes was an explosives expert and a fervent Catholic. King James I and his advisers were unpopular as they were forcing Catholics to pay fines for practising their religion. The plot was to take barrels of gunpowder into the cellars below the Houses of Parliament and to blow up the building when King James was visiting Parliament. Guy Fawkes hid himself in the cellar and his job was to light the fuse on the barrels of gunpowder. However, the plotters were betrayed, the cellars searched and Guy Fawkes was found. He was taken and tortured before finally being burned to death.

Preparation
Make a tinderbox from a metal box containing a piece of flintstone and piece of steel, together with some straw and some small pieces of cloth.

Resources needed
Tinderbox, lantern (which the soldiers would use for searching the cellars). Pencils, crayons and felt-tipped pens, pictures of Guy Fawkes and the Houses of Parliament.

What to do
Introduction
Talk about what happens each year on November 5th. Children may have been to firework displays and be able to talk about what they have seen and heard. They may have been to bonfires and burned a Guy or seen children collecting money for a Guy on the streets. Sing the rhyme:
Remember, remember the 5th of November,
Gunpowder, treason and plot,
I see no reason why gunpowder treason
Should ever be forgot.
Explain that treason means plotting against the king and that they are going to hear a story about this.
Development
Explain to the children the problem the Catholics had of wanting to worship in their own way, but having to pay a lot of money to do this. What solutions can the children suggest? Explain the solution planned by Guy Fawkes and his friends. Refer to any additional pictures of Guy Fawkes and the Houses of Parliament available from your resources.

Talk about Guy Fawkes' job to light the fuse of the gunpowder. There were no matches. Show the children the tinderbox and try to make a spark by striking the flint stone against the steel. The spark would then set alight the cloth or straw.

Discuss what Guy Fawkes might have been feeling as he heard the steps of the people searching the cellar. Perhaps he hoped that they would not find him if he kept very quiet and still. Talk about the people looking for Guy Fawkes – were they nervous? Did they think they would really find him?

Ask the children their views on the story. Do they think that Guy Fawkes was a good or a bad man? Was it right to plot to kill a lot of people? Why do they think we have celebrated this event for nearly 400 years?
Conclusion
Ask the children to take on the role of Guy Fawkes and to write his own version of the events.

Suggestion(s) for extension
Encourage the children to explore the feelings of other characters in the story. What did the King feel when he heard of the plot? What were the soldiers' feelings as they searched for Guy and when they found him? Children can find pictures of the present Houses of Parliament and the Queen attending the state opening.

Suggestion(s) for support
Instead of writing, children may like to draw their own pictures to illustrate the story. Alternatively, children might like to re-tell the story in role-play. Convert the play area into the cellars where Guy Fawkes hid. Provide props such as lanterns for the soldiers and for Guy Fawkes, a tinder-box and pieces of thick string to represent fuses, cloaks and hats.

Assessment opportunities
Can the children re-tell the story in the correct sequence? Can the children explain why the Gunpowder Plot was hatched? Listen to children's comments about the ways in which the plot is commemorated.

Opportunities for IT

Children could use a word processor to undertake some of the short writing tasks associated with this activity. For example they could write a single statement about whether Guy Fawkes was a good or bad man, or their feelings of different people involved in the plot. Print out individual statements and use these as part of a class display.

Children could use an art package to experiment with colour-mixing skills using the computer. They could draw their own fire with different shaped flames and different colours. Print out the work and collage it together to form a background for other writing on the subject. Alternatively children could design their own firework pattern using an art package. This might involve them in drawing sparks and firework shapes, colouring them and then copying them and moving them to new positions on the screen to create a symmetrical firework pattern.

Display ideas

Develop children's colour-mixing skills using orange, red and yellow paint. Ask them to completely cover a sheet of paper with shades of these paints. Once the paint is dry, cut out the paper into flame shapes. Create a large bonfire frieze using the flame shapes. Dress a Guy in different materials and place on the top of the bonfire. Label the display with the bonfire rhyme, '*Remember, remember the 5th of November*'. Display the children's writing alongside the bonfire.

KING ARTHUR AND THE KNIGHTS OF THE ROUND TABLE

To learn about the legend of King Arthur. To explore how versions of stories can change as they are told by different storytellers.

✝✝ *Whole class. Groups.*

🕐 *Whole class introduction 20 minutes; development 20 minutes; groups 30 minutes.*

Previous skills/knowledge needed

This activity will draw on children's abilities to role-play.

Key background information

The legend of King Arthur appeared in *The History of the Kings of Britain* by Geoffrey of Monmouth, who wrote in the first half of the twelfth century. Geoffrey probably based his account of King Arthur on different stories which had been handed down orally through different generations. According to Geoffrey, Arthur was a great king and war leader who had fought the Saxon invaders in the fifth century AD. The legend of Arthur was developed subsequently by medieval poets and storytellers. The exploits of Arthur and his knights of the Round Table epitomised the age of chivalry and exemplified the qualities to which medieval knights should aspire. Knights were expected to be fearless and to fight bravely in battle. They were meant to be chivalrous and gentle to ladies of noble birth.

There are several versions of the story of how Arthur became king. One story describes how Arthur was stolen away from his royal parents by the magician, Merlin when he was a baby. As Arthur's father, the king, lay dying, knights from all over the kingdom came to the royal palace, claiming to be the next heir. Merlin magically sealed a sword in a stone and all claimants were invited to try and remove it. No-one was able to do this, until an unknown young man (Arthur) stepped forward and effortlessly pulled the sword out. Arthur was then acknowledged as the next king.

Preparation

Gather together some props which the children might use for their role-playing activity. Include: swords; cloaks; crowns; magician's hat.

Resources needed

Pictures and books about King Arthur and medieval knights. Role-play props.

What to do

Introduction

Talk about the different ways we can find out about what happened in the past, including writing, pictures, objects and buildings. Mention 'people talking about what happened' as a good source of information. Explain how people often elaborate or change part of a story as they tell it.

Play Chinese Whispers with the children. Sit in a circle and whisper a message to a child sitting next to you. The child can then pass the message on to his/her neighbour. When the message has been passed around the circle, compare its final version with the starting version. Are there any differences? Has anybody changed the original message?

Development

Tell the children that they are going to learn about King Arthur. Stories about him have changed as they have been told, just as the message changed in the game of Chinese Whispers. Children might be familiar with some of the stories about Arthur from television, film and books. Discuss what they already know about him and explain how the first stories were written using the background information.

Re-tell the story about how Arthur was stolen as a baby away from his parents. You could add the things which Arthur was probably taught during his childhood for example: how to ride and fight with a sword; hunting and falconry; serving at table and playing a musical instrument. Refer to books and pictures if available about medieval knights. Tell the children what happened as Arthur's father lay dying and how Arthur eventually became king.

Conclusion

Organise the children into groups of four or five children. Ask the children to re-tell the story of how Arthur became king by acting it out. They will need to think of which characters to include and who is going to play them. Children will also need to consider if they need any props to help them tell the story. They might choose to make some for themselves. Ask the children to watch each others' versions

of the story and to compare them. Have groups included any different details? Remind children that versions of stories change as they are told and ask them to look for differences in the versions.

Suggestion(s) for extension

Children can research more information about King Arthur and his knights. They might choose to write their own stories for a book about Arthur and the Knights of the Round Table. Suitable plots which the children could develop might include: rescuing maidens; fighting against terrible monsters and wicked rulers; attacking castles; sieges using battering rams and giant catapults.

Suggestion(s) for support

Children can engage with the role-play activity according to their different abilities and stages of maturity.

Assessment opportunities

Ask the children their views on whether Arthur really existed. Can they suggest any reasons to support their views? Do they recognise that films and story books provide different representations of the story of Arthur?

Opportunities for IT

Children could use a CD-ROM to search for other information about King Arthur and his Knights. They could compare these stories to those from other sources of information.

Display ideas

Ask children to research medieval costume and to draw and colour their own medieval knights in armour seated around a Round Table. Some children might choose to draw the knights' ladies too. Alternatively create a life-size figure of King Arthur. Draw around a child lying down and use silver foil for King Arthur's armour. Add a sword and shield for King Arthur to hold.

MARY SEACOLE

To learn about Mary Seacole's work and about aspects of nursing and hospital life in the nineteenth century. To sequence different episodes in Mary Seacole's life in chronological order.

†† *Whole class; pairs/individuals.*

🕐 *Whole class 20 minutes; pairs/individuals 40 minutes.*

Previous skills/knowledge needed

This activity will draw on children's ability to sequence stories.

Key background information

Mary Seacole was born in Jamaica in 1805. She was the daughter of a West Indian nurse and a Scottish soldier who was serving in the West Indies. Mary Seacole learned a lot about medicine from her mother who set up a hotel to care for sick people in Jamaica. In 1853 Britain became involved in a war with Russia and sent soldiers over to the Crimea. There were heavy casualties. Many soldiers died from their wounds and diseases rather than on the battlefield.

Mary Seacole wanted to help these men so she sold her hotel in Jamaica and travelled to England. She approached the War Office in London and offered to help with her medical experience. Her offer was rejected by the War Office so Mary Seacole travelled to the Crimea at her own expense. She established The British Hotel to care for the sick and injured soldiers and also visited the soldiers with supplies of food and medicine in their camp and on the battlefield. *The Times* war correspondent praised her work and her bravery amongst the troops in his reports home. When she returned to England after the war, Mary was awarded two medals for bravery. She wrote a book about her life called, *The Wonderful Adventures of Mrs Seacole in Many Lands*. A fund was started to collect money to support her in old age. She died in 1881 in relative obscurity.

Preparation

Prepare enough of the photocopiable sheet on page 144 for each child. Fold paper to make small books with six pages where children can stick their pictures of Mary Seacole.

Resources needed

Pictures of Mary Seacole. Props to help tell the story: Mary Seacole's bag which she carried with her when she visited the soldiers on the battle field (containing bandages and swabs); a bonnet and cloak. The photocopiable sheet on page 144, crayons, felt-tipped pens and pencils, adhesive, scissors. Small books containing six pages for the story of Mary Seacole.

What to do

Introduction

Begin by talking about the work of doctors and nurses. Discuss the importance of hygiene to prevent disease and the use of antiseptics.

Development

Use the background information to tell the children the story of Mary Seacole. Dress one child as Mary Seacole with her bag of medicines and bandages to stimulate the children's interest in her story. The story provides many opportunities for including details about ways of life in the past, for example the care of the sick and wounded. Before antiseptics many soldiers died of their wounds. Cholera reached epidemic proportions due to lack of knowledge about the importance of a fresh water supply.

In 1973 a group of nurses from Jamaica commemorated Mary Seacole by erecting a gravestone in St Mary's Catholic Cemetery, Harrow Road, London. Ask the children if they think it is important to remember her. How else are people who have lived in the past remembered?

The wonderful adventures of Mary Seacole

▲ Cut out the pictures and place them in the correct sequence to tell the story of Mary Seacole.

▲ Draw you own picture in the empty box to add to the story.

Conclusion

Hand out photocopiable page 144 to each child and ask the children to cut out the pictures. Working in pairs, ask the children to sequence the pictures in the correct order and to explain what is happening in the story. In the empty box provided on the sheet, ask the children to draw their own picture to add to the story of Mary Seacole.

Ask the children to glue the correct sequence into the prepared books. Invite the children to design their own cover for *The Wonderful Adventures of Mary Seacole*.

Suggestion(s) for extension

Children can write the story of Mary Seacole beneath the pictures. Ask them to try and explain why Mary Seacole wanted to help the soldiers. Encourage children to find out more about medical conditions at the time. Children can also find out about the life of Mary Seacole's contemporary, Florence Nightingale.

Suggestion(s) for support

Pair children needing support with more able children or organise the sequencing activity as a whole group or class activity. Reduce the number of pictures for the children to put in sequence.

Assessment opportunities

Can the children tell the story in the correct sequence? What information can the children recount about hospitals and the care of the sick in the past?

Opportunities for IT

Children could use suitable word processor or desktop publishing software to create a simple newspaper about Mary Seacole's life and work. Different groups could write about different parts of the story.

If the word processor is set up in advance with narrower columns for the print these can be printed out and then stuck onto a newspaper format to create a class newspaper.

If suitable DTP software is available a newspaper format can be set up in advance by the teacher and children can then come to the computer and write in their own parts of the story. The completed paper can then be printed out.

Children could also use a CD-ROM to look up information about Mary Seacole and Florence Nightingale. Similarities and differences could be discussed as a part of this work.

Display ideas

Create your own British Hotel in the classroom. Plenty of bandages and materials for washing wounds will be needed. Include beds and dressing-up clothes for the soldiers and Mary Seacole.

Reference to photocopiable sheet

The photocopiable page 144 shows incidents in the life of Mary Seacole. The pictures are: her as a child with her mother in Jamaica; Mary on board ship, (children can place this as either Mary Seacole crossing the Atlantic from Jamaica or travelling to the Crimea); Mary talking to the officials at the war office; Mary looking after the soldiers; Mary receiving her medal on her return to England.

HIGHWAY ROBBERS: DICK TURPIN

To examine travel in the past and to learn about the past through stories of well-known personalities.
†† *Whole class; individuals.*
🕐 *Whole class 30 minutes; individuals 20 minutes.*

Previous skills/knowledge needed

Knowledge about roads and road transport in the past. See pages 71–72. Ability to role-play different situations.

Key background information

Roads were dangerous places in the past; during the eighteenth century for example coaches used to travel so slowly that they were an easy target for robbery. People tried to guard themselves against robbery by carrying weapons such as pistols and muskets.

Staging inns provided refreshments and overnight stopping places. Sometimes the innkeepers were in touch

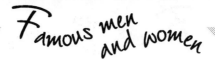

with local highway robbers and would let them know if they had any wealthy travellers staying with them.

One of the most celebrated highway robbers was Dick Turpin (1706-1739). He worked with a gang of thieves robbing country farmhouses and then became a horse thief. Whilst trying to avoid capture he shot his accomplice Tom King by mistake. Dick Turpin conducted many highway robberies and is claimed to have made a record-breaking ride from London to York on his famous horse Black Bess. The horse is said to have died from exhaustion and lies commemorated by a plaque on York race course. Eventually Turpin was captured, imprisoned in York castle and found guilty of many crimes.

Not all highway robbers were men; Moll Cutpurse was a renowned robber who held up carriages on the road.

Preparation
Photocopy page 145 for each child, background information about the condition of roads in the eighteenth century for establishing the context of the story (see pages 91–92).

Resources needed
Pictures of old coaches and coaching inns; people in eighteenth century dress, including some highway robbers. Clothing props: masks and dark cloaks for the highway robbers; purses with money and jewels for the travellers. Children to act: four children seated as if in a carriage; one child at the front as the driver; two children to act as highway robbers; an innkeeper. Photocopiable sheet on page 145.

What to do
Set the scene for the highway drama by providing the children with information about road transport in the past and the conditions of the roads. Use the background information to help tell the story of an imaginary highway robbery using the children. Provide the selected children with an identity and a particular role in the story. Encourage the children to role-play their different parts as you tell the story. After the story

has been told, ask the different characters to re-tell the story from their own point of view. Where were the travellers in the carriage going? What valuables did they have? When did they first notice that the carriage had been held up? What were their feelings when they heard the highway robber cry, 'Stand and deliver?'. The highway robbers could explain how they knew a coach would be coming along their road; where they had been waiting and for how long.

Hand out the photocopiable sheets and ask the children to draw a wanted poster for their highway robber. Name the robber. Describe what he/she has done and offer a reward for his/her capture.

Suggestion(s) for extension
Working in a group children can write the story of the highway robbery from the points of view of the different characters. A book can be made recording the different characters' accounts of the event.

Suggestion(s) for support
If necessary you could limit the activity to drawing pictures of the highway robbers.

Assessment opportunities
Can the children recount the story of a highway robbery? Do they recognise any differences between travelling now and in the past?

Opportunities for IT
Children could use an art or drawing package to make their own 'wanted' posters for Dick Turpin. They could be shown how to use simple drawing tools and how to add text, move it into the correct position, select appropriate fonts etc.

They could also use a word processor for this task, choosing suitable font styles and sizes to get their messages across. They might also need to be shown how to centre text using the centre command rather than positioning text by adding spaces. Pictures could be added either from an art package or drawn by hand and stuck on once the textual part has been printed out.

▲ Complete the Wanted for Highway Robbery Poster.

Highway robbery

WANTED

FOR HIGHWAY ROBBERY

REWARD

Display ideas
The 'wanted' posters can be displayed in a rogues' gallery. Provide props in the classroom for children to role-play a highway robbery in the classroom.

Reference to photocopiable sheet
The photocopiable page 145 provides an outline of a 'wanted for highway' robbery poster for the children to complete.

 GRACE DARLING

To learn the story of Grace Darling's rescue of survivors from a nineteenth century shipwreck. They will discuss different people's accounts of the rescue and share ideas on how and whether Grace should be remembered.

†† *Whole class/individual.*

🕑 *Whole class 25 minutes; individual 15 minutes.*

Previous skills/knowledge needed
This activity draws on children's background knowledge of the lifeboat service and safety at sea.

Key background information
Grace Darling was the daughter of a lighthouse keeper living on one of the Farne islands off the coast of Northumberland. Early one morning in September 1838, Grace (who was 22 years old) awoke to the sight of a steamer being wrecked off one of the islands. *The Forfarshire* had hit some rocks in the storm during the night and was breaking up. A few

survivors were standing huddled on the rocks above the ship. A terrible storm was raging, but Grace and her father decided to attempt to rescue the survivors. They launched their boat and rowed across to the wreck. The nine survivors crowded into the boat and were rowed back to the lighthouse. Here they were fed, and able to change into dry clothes in the very cramped conditions of the lighthouse. A lifeboat was also launched from Sunderland on the mainland to rescue the survivors of the *Forfarshire*, but arrived after the Darlings. The lifeboat men subsequently sought refuge in the Darling's lighthouse until the storm subsided.

Grace's courage in the rescue was recorded and she became nationally famous. The Shipwreck Institution (later to become the Royal National Lifeboat Institute) awarded Grace and her father William, a silver medal to record their bravery. The Shipwreck Institution had been founded in 1824 with the aim to provide a national rescue service for saving lives at sea.

Grace Darling's act of bravery captured the imagination of people at the time and she was inundated with gifts. Visitors came to the lighthouse and artists painted scenes of the wreck and Grace's dramatic rescue. People wrote to Grace asking for samples of her handwriting or a cutting from her hair. In comparison, the bravery of the lifeboatmen who had rowed for five hours to reach the wreck went largely unnoticed and they only received a very small reward for their bravery.

Preparation
Make a collection of books about lifeboats and nineteenth-century ships.

Resources needed
Pictures and books about lifeboats, pictures of nineteenth-century ships and Grace Darling. Pencils, crayons and felt-tipped pens.

What to do
Introduction
Talk about dangers at sea. What happens when a ship is in distress? Discuss the work of the life boat service and the rescue work they undertake. Talk about the equipment and the sort of boats used. Explain the purpose of lighthouses to warn ships of approaching dangers.

Development

Set the context of a dark, stormy morning with the wind blowing hard and re-tell the story of Grace Darling using the background information above. Ask the children if they think she was very brave. How would they have rewarded her? Refer to pictures of nineteenth-century ships, if available, from your resources so the children can imagine the scene of the shipwreck more vividly.

Conclusion

Ask the children to design a medal to present to Grace Darling. How would they choose to illustrate it? Would the children have rewarded the lifeboatmen as well? Do the children think it is important to remember Grace Darling?

Suggestion(s) for extension

Children can write the story as a newspaper report. Ask them to compose a headline for a report of the dramatic rescue. There are opportunities to use IT for the newsprint.

Suggestion(s) for support

Children can respond to the story at different levels according to their abilities and stages of maturity.

Assessment opportunities

Can the children re-tell the story of Grace Darling's rescue? Use drama for children to re-enact the story and listen to their comments. Can they imagine how people might have felt at the time?

Opportunities for IT

Children could use a word processor or desktop publishing package to write a newspaper report of the rescue. A newspaper format could be set up in advance so that children could concentrate on their writing rather than the layout of the page. Alternatively groups of children could design their own page.

A similar activity can be undertaken with just a word processor, by setting the line length to around 30 characters so that children's writing is in a narrow column. Once printed

out the columns can be stuck onto a larger sheet to make a newspaper –style layout. Children could also use a drawing or art package to design a medal for Grace Darling.

Display ideas

Create a display depicting Grace Darling's rescue. Use different pieces of torn blue, green, black and white tissue to create a stormy sea and use dark paints for the sky. Add pictures of Grace and her father in the boat, the wreck, rocks and the lighthouse stuck onto small boxes or tabs to create a three-dimensional effect.

SAMUEL PLIMSOLL

To learn about aspects of Victorian life through the work of Samuel Plimsoll. To find out why the Plimsoll load-line was introduced and the results of this decision.

†† *Whole class; pairs/individuals.*

🕓 *Whole class 20 minutes; pairs/individuals 15 minutes.*

Previous skills/knowledge needed

Children will need to have had experience with floating and sinking objects in water.

Key background information

Samuel Plimsoll (1824 -1898) was a Member of Parliament for Derby from 1868-1880. He was particularly concerned with the safety of merchant seaman and sought to introduce laws which would protect them and make their ships more seaworthy. Victorian seamen faced many dangers; unscrupulous ship owners would insist that their ships were heavily loaded so that they could carry as much cargo as possible. Such 'coffin ships' were very unsafe and many ships were lost due to overloading. However, the ship owners did not bear any losses since they were able to insure their ships and re-coup the full value of the vessels lost. They had no obligations to pay compensation for the loss of life of their seamen. Seamen who did complain and who refused to work on dangerous ships could be accused of breaking their contracts and faced terms of imprisonment. If they dared to protest it was unlikely that they would ever be hired to work on ships again.

Samuel Plimsoll publicised the injustice of such practices. He travelled the country attending meetings and published some papers. Plimsoll introduced several bills into the House of Commons to protect the seamen and met with stiff opposition. The Merchant Shipping Act (1876) established the requirement for a load-line which was to be a circular disc, 12 inches in diameter with a horizontal line, 18 inches in length going through its centre. However, individual ship owners had to be responsible for fixing the lines on their

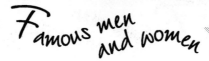

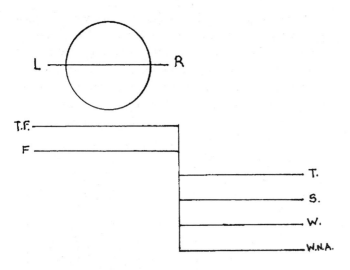

children to express their views on the Victorian ship owners and on the work of Samuel Plimsoll.

Conclusion

In pairs, ask the children to draw their own Plimsoll line on a boat in the water tray, using waterproof markers. Having marked the boat, the children can ask another pair of children to test whether they have placed their Plimsoll line at the right level. Children can check whether the Plimsoll line provides an accurate gauge for different sorts of cargoes.

Suggestion(s) for extension

Children could pretend they are a Victorian seaman and write to Samuel Plimsoll describing some of the dangers which they have met at sea.

Suggestion(s) for support

Children could observe the effects of overloading on boats which have Plimsoll lines already marked on.

Assessment opportunities

Can the children explain what Samuel Plimsoll achieved? Can they talk about any ways in which the Plimsoll line changed people's lives in Victorian times?

Display ideas

A large diagram showing the markings of the Plimsoll load-line could be drawn for the children to refer to.

ships and it was not until they became the responsibility of the Board of Trade, 14 years later, that such lines became really reliable. The markings of the Plimsoll load-line were finally agreed in 1933. Different lines indicate the limit of submergence according to water density. Tropical Fresh (TF) and Fresh (F), and in salt water, Tropical (T), Summer (S), Winter (W) and Winter North Atlantic (WNA).

Preparation

Prepare the classroom for water play. Make a large poster showing the markings of the Plimsoll load-line.

Resources needed

Water tray filled with water; different boats; waterproof markers; small objects which can be used as cargo such as marbles, building bricks, counters and shells. Poster showing the Plimsoll load-line.

What to do

Introduction

Load some boats in the water tray with different cargoes and watch what happens to them. Do all the boats float? What makes some of the boats sink? Ask the children what sort of cargoes real ships carry today. What do they think would happen if a ship was overloaded? How do sailors know when a ship is full? Talk about the Plimsoll line and how it works.

Development

Tell the children the story of the Plimsoll line. Encourage the

QUEEN ELIZABETH I

To find out about the life of Queen Elizabeth I from a range of sources and information.

†† *Group working in pairs, then individual.*

🕐 *Group 20 minutes; individuals 40 minutes.*

Previous skills/knowledge needed

This activity requires the children to make close observations of different portraits of Queen Elizabeth I.

Key background information

Queen Elizabeth I was the daughter of Henry VIII and Anne Boleyn. She was born in 1533 and died in 1603. Elizabeth became queen following the deaths of her younger half-brother, Edward VI and elder half-sister, Mary. In her portraits Queen Elizabeth I is painted wearing magnificent clothes and jewels to demonstrate her importance and power. Particular features were often included in the portraits to symbolise her greatness. For example: the globe signified Queen Elizabeth I's expanding empire; the rainbow – an emblem of peace after a storm; the serpent symbolised wisdom. She

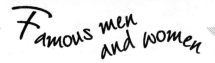

had a huge wardrobe of clothes and accessories such as fans, gloves, hats, muffs. Many were presents from courtiers trying to maintain her favours. The dresses were elaborately embroidered with different threads and jewels.

Queen Elizabeth I's hair was a reddish-gold colour and as she grew older she wore a variety of wigs. She cleaned her teeth with a tooth-cloth and a toothpick, but her teeth decayed badly. One visitor recorded that they were yellow, another that they were black, this was attributed to the Queen's love of sugar. There is also a description that she stuffed her cheeks with fine cloths to hide the hollows and wrinkles. Queen Elizabeth I painted her face with strange lotions which probably included a mixture of egg white, powdered eggshell, alum, borax and poppy seeds. Appearance was important for her: in 1596 an order from the Privy Council commanded that all portraits which were to her 'great offence' should be destroyed. She was an accomplished scholar. She studied Greek, Latin, French and Italian. She enjoyed dancing and music.

Preparation
Collect portraits of Queen Elizabeth I from books, posters and postcards.

Resources needed
Different portraits of Queen Elizabeth I. Magnifying glasses. Large sheets of paper. Pencils, crayons, felt-tipped pens and painting materials.

What to do
Working in pairs ask the children to select a portrait of Queen Elizabeth I and to talk about what they can see. When they have given their initial impressions, focus some of their observations more tightly. Ask, what is she wearing? Encourage the children to describe her clothes and jewels. What is her facial expression like? Is she happy, sad? What sort of impression of a queen does the picture give? Do the children think that Queen Elizabeth I really looked like the portrait painter has presented her? What is happening in the background of the picture? Is this important? Ask each pair of children to report to a larger group and talk about the things which they have found out. Use the background information to provide the children with more information about the queen and her wardrobe.

Using the large sheets of paper ask the children to draw and paint their own portrait of Queen Elizabeth I. Encourage them to include details which they have noticed on the portraits which they have observed. When the paintings are dry, frame them and create a portrait gallery of Queen Elizabeth I.

Suggestion(s) for extension
Children can write a guide for their portrait gallery to include details about the portraits and the clothes. Children might like to investigate other Elizabethan portraits and use them as a source of information about the clothing of rich people at the time. They could look closely at particular patterns of the cloth and try and copy a segment of the cloth's design. Children could also look at some of the miniature pictures which were painted during the Elizabethan period.

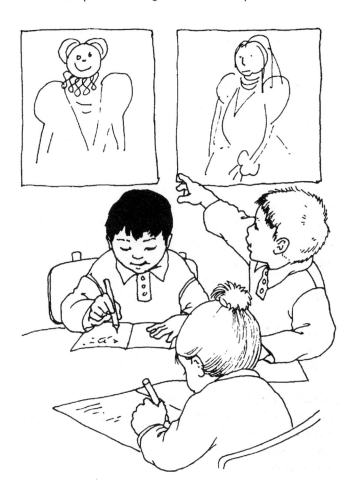

Suggestion(s) for support
Some children might find if helpful to be provided with an outline of a face as a starting point for their portraits.

Assessment opportunities
Do the children make detailed observations of the portraits? Are they able to use the portraits as sources of information to say what the clothes of rich people were like during Elizabethan times?

Opportunities for IT
Children could use a word processor to write labels for their portraits, giving some extra background information about Queen Elizabeth I. The children could experiment with different font styles to ensure that their labels can be read from a distance.

Display ideas
Use the pictures to create an Elizabethan portrait gallery.

ST HILDA

To learn about the life of St Hilda through stories.

†† *Whole class; individuals.*

🕐 *Whole class 20 minutes. Individuals 20 minutes.*

Previous skills/knowledge needed
This activity will draw on children's handwriting skills.

Key background information
St Hilda (614-80) provides a good example of how in the Anglo-Saxon church a woman could attain great influence and authority. She was a member of the Northumbrian royal family and lived a secular life until she was 33. She then founded a small religious house on the banks of the river Wear and from there moved on to be abbess of Hartlepool and later, Whitby. Both Hartlepool and Whitby were double monasteries, accommodating both monks and nuns.

St Hilda became renowned as a scholar, and Whitby with its library, was acknowledged as a seat of learning. Kings and nobles also sought her advice. At the Synod of Whitby 664, hosted by Hilda, important lay people and clerics agreed to adopt the Roman calendar for calculating the date of Easter. At this time books were precious possessions and the various skills of calligraphers, artists and jewellers in monasteries were needed for their production. The Bible, in particular the gospels, was copied out carefully onto either parchment (sheepskin) or vellum (calf skin) using goose quill pens. Book covers were often richly decorated and covered in jewels.

Some of the most famous gospels, for example the Lindisfarne Gospels, were copied out in around 700, shortly following Hilda's death. Hilda is also reputed to have encouraged vernacular literature. Caedmon was a herdsman who lived in the double monastery at Whitby. In a dream he was ordered to sing the story of the Creation. The story was told to Hilda who encouraged him to compose other hymns and poems on biblical themes. The buildings at Whitby were sacked by the Vikings in the raid about 800, but the medieval remains of the abbey can still be seen today.

Illuminated letter from the Lindisfarne Gospels

Preparation
Collect some examples of different illuminated manuscripts. Prepare enough copies of the photocopiable sheet on page 146 for each child.

Resources needed
Photocopiable page 146, examples of different illuminated manuscripts, felt-tipped pens.

What to do
Introduction
Begin by talking about saints. Do the children know what sort of people became saints? Can they think of any names of saints? Do they know why these people were made saints? Tell the children that they are going to hear the story of St Hilda who was made a saint because she lived a holy life and told people about God. Talk about what living a holy life might mean for example praying, helping other people, being kind to others and making people better. Ask the children to contribute their ideas.

Development

Use the background information to tell the children about St Hilda. You will probably need to explain what monasteries were. Explain how St Hilda encouraged the collection and making of books. Talk about how books were made in Anglo-Saxon times and encourage children to recognise the amount of time they took to produce. This could be contrasted with printed books today. If possible, look at some of the illuminated letters and manuscripts collected in the resources. Encourage children to look carefully at the designs and to describe what they can see.

Conclusion

Hand out the photocopiable sheet of the illuminated manuscripts. Talk about the different designs and features in the illuminated letters. The children can colour in the detail.

Suggestion(s) for extension

Children could look for Anglo-Saxon designs from other sources of evidence for example church crosses, jewellery, sword hilts. They could try to copy some of these designs.

Children could research other saints, finding out who they were, what they did and why they have been remembered. They could compile a class book of different saints from the information which they have gathered.

Suggestion(s) for support

Some children might find the photocopiable sheet too detailed to colour in. Use the sheet as a source of information and ask the children to design a special pattern around their own initial letters.

Assessment opportunities

Can the children talk about some of the reasons why St Hilda has been remembered?

Display ideas

Make your own scriptorium in the classroom. Equip the play area with sharpened goose quills and/or thin paintbrushes.

Provide washable inks and different sorts of paper. Children might like to dress up in simple monks' or nuns' habits before they go in to write. Have examples from other illuminated letters around for reference. Some children may enjoy making jewelled covers for the books from card and pieces of shiny paper. Pin dark coloured sugar paper to the wall and cut out thin window shapes with semi-circular arches at the top.

Reference to photocopiable sheet

The photocopiable sheet on page 146 shows an example of an illuminated letter from the Lindisfarne Gospels.

McADAM'S ROADS

To learn about the work of a famous engineer, John McAdam and the development of roadbuilding techniques. To understand how these developments affected people's way of life.

†† *Whole class; pairs; whole class.*

🕐 *Whole class 20 minutes; pairs 10 minutes to design and test a road; whole class 20 minutes discussion.*

Previous skills/knowledge needed

Knowledge of different roads and road building from books and stories and/or personal experience.

Key background information

Travelling by road was not easy in the past. The network of Roman roads fell into disrepair during the Middle Ages. Most roads were not surfaced and became muddy tracks after any rainfall. They were often full of deep ruts and potholes. Obstructions such as fallen down trees would sometimes block the road. Roads were often dangerous; there is an account of someone falling off a carriage and drowning in a very deep rut. Overhanging trees could sweep people seated on the top of the carriage off onto the road. Local parishes were responsible for the upkeep of roads in their area, but did not always fulfil their obligations and many roads were in a very bad state of repair. Turnpike trusts were established in the eighteenth century to build and repair roads. Travellers paid tolls at turnpikes or toll-bars to travel on these roads. New techniques for road building were gradually developed. John McAdam (1756–1836) emphasised the importance of good drainage. He made roads which were higher in the centre so that the water would drain to the sides. McAdam made a road by laying three layers of small broken stones on the earth. Carriage wheels packed the stones together as they travelled over them and made a strong surface. This process was called by some people, 'macadamising'. He became surveyor-general of Bristol roads in 1815, and later of the whole country in 1827, which provided him with opportunities for implementing his ideas on a large scale.

Thomas Telford (1757-1834) also used small stones for surfacing roads. He also insisted on laying firm foundations with large stones on the bottom layer. The better road surfaces enabled speedier travel on the roads and encouraged more travellers.

Preparation
Prepare different trays containing sand, stones and gravel.

Resources needed
Different trays containing sand, stones and gravel. Spare tray, sieves. A selection of toy vehicles. Pictures and books of modern road building and of road travel in the eighteenth and nineteenth centuries.

What to do
Introduction
Talk about the different roads which children have travelled on, for example, country lanes; main roads; dual carriageways and motorways. Discuss the speed of different vehicles and the amount of traffic on the roads. Ask the children to describe different road surfaces, for example smooth; tarred; sloping so that rainwater does not collect on the surface. Children might have seen some road-building in operation. What machines are used? How are new roads built? Refer to books and pictures from the resources if available.

Development
Use the background information to tell the children what roads were like before McAdam. Talk about the improvements he made in road building. If available, look at some of the pictures of eighteenth and early nineteenth century roads and the sort of vehicles which they carried. Explain that the better roads made journeys quicker, safer and more comfortable for travellers.

Conclusion
In pairs ask the children to make roads from the materials in the different trays. Ask the children to investigate which material makes the best surface and to test the roads using the toy vehicles. Invite the pairs of children to talk about their investigations with the whole class.

Suggestion(s) for extension
Children can draw plans and diagrams to provide instructions on how to build a good road. Children could research other great road builders of the past and investigate how they built their roads, for example the Romans.

Suggestion(s) for support
This activity provides opportunities for children to respond at different levels according to their abilities and stages of development.

Assessment opportunities
Can children recognise some of the advantages of having a better system of road building?

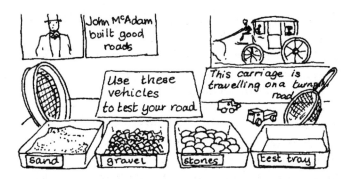

Display ideas
Create an interactive display with trays filled with different materials. Provide different sieves so that the materials can be separated for other children to work with. Encourage children to design, construct and test their own roads. Provide opportunities for them to record their investigations in different ways.

JOHN LOGIE BAIRD

To learn about a famous inventor and investigate how his invention has affected lifestyles over a period of time.

†† *Whole class and individuals.*

⊕ *Introductory session variable; development 25 minutes; conclusion 25 minutes.*

Previous skill/knowledge needed
Children will be able to use their knowledge of television and television programmes.

Key background information
John Logie Baird was born in 1888 in Helensburgh, near Glasgow, the son of a local minister. From a very young age he enjoyed experimenting. At home in his bedroom he rigged up a telephone exchange and connected wires across the streets to the homes of some of his friends. He also wired

up his parents' home to receive electricity and built his own generator run by a water wheel under the kitchen tap which supplied a set of batteries. As a child, he was also interested in photography and formed his own photographic club.

Baird qualified as an electrical engineer and for many years worked in jobs that didn't satisfy him, while at the same time he continued to experiment and invent things. Among his inventions was a thermostatic sock that kept feet warm in winter and cool in summer. He also invented pneumatic soles for shoes but the soles burst when he tested them.

In 1923, Baird conceived the idea of 'seeing by wireless', and worked out a system for transmitting pictures by wireless waves (or television). He got his materials from scrapyards, (radio valves etc.). He obtained a tea chest, biscuit tin, hat box and some knitting needles. With glue, sealing wax and string, Baird rigged up his apparatus. He made a circular scanner from the top of the hat box and cut holes around the edge. A cardboard cross was placed in bright light in front of the scanner and as the scanner revolved, the shadow of the cross was transmitted on to a white sheet behind.

Baird worked hard to perfect his invention. He gave daily demonstrations in a London store. In 1929 the BBC took up his invention and staged an experimental broadcast of two men talking. Baird's scanner did not transmit very clear pictures and his invention was improved by the Marconi company and Electrical Musical Instruments (EMI) who devised an electronic system with sharper pictures. This system was adopted by the BBC in 1937. Baird died in 1946.

Television was gradually becoming more popular. The coronation of Queen Elizabeth II in 1953 was televised and watched by millions. Many people bought television sets for the occasion. Colour TV was introduced in Britain in 1967.

Preparation

Prepare the photocopiable sheet on page 147 for each child in the class.

Resources needed

Pencils, paper, colouring materials, photocopiable page 147.

What to do

Introduction

Talk to the children about television. How many children have a set at home? What sorts of programmes do they watch? Do they have any favourite programmes? When do they enjoy watching television? Children can conduct a survey into class viewing habits or favourite programmes. There are opportunities for using IT to record and present their findings.

Development

Discuss how children amused themselves before the widespread use of television. The children may think of: playing games; listening to the wireless; going to the cinema. Discuss how television has changed people's lives, for example, being able to watch sporting events at home; seeing pictures of different places in the world; watching news and great events, being entertained at home, rather than going out. Use the background information to tell the story of John Logie Baird and his different inventions. Talk about how television became more and more popular, especially after the coronation.

Conclusion

Hand out the photocopiable sheet to each child. Ask them to think of reasons for buying the television set and to produce an advert encouraging people to buy the set in the picture.

Suggestion(s) for extension

Children can ask parents and older members of their families what programmes they enjoyed watching when they were children. Did they enjoy similar programmes? Did all families own television sets? Children can be encouraged to devise their own questionnaire to take home with similar questions.

Suggestion(s) for support

Some children might find difficulty writing the advertisement slogan. Alternatively, use the photocopiable sheet for children to record the differences between a 1930s TV set and a modern one. Ask the children to look carefully at the picture of the 1930s set and to draw a picture of a modern television set showing their favourite programme beneath. Encourage them to talk about the differences which they can see.

Assessment opportunities

Can children suggest ways in which television has changed people's lives? Are they able to imagine what life without television might have been like?

Opportunities for IT

Ask the children to collect data about different televisions, favourite programmes or time spent watching TV. The data could be recorded using a database or presented graphically using graphing software.

Focus on some very specific questions. Where there are only two elements of data, such as a quiz show and number of viewers, it is easy for children to enter this information

into simple graphing software which enables them to show the data in a bar or pie chart. It is also important that they interpret the information and are given opportunities to discuss the benefits of using software for this type of work.

Children could also use a word processor to write their advertising slogan (see photocopiable sheet). This will give the children opportunities to draft and redraft their work. Once they have composed the slogan they can choose a font, alter the size and even add colour to it.

Display ideas

Cut out paper in the shape of television screens and ask children to draw a picture to show on the screen for example, an incident from the life of Baird. Alternatively, provide the children with books showing aspects of life from the 1930s and ask them to complete a scene, paying attention to the different fashions which people were wearing. Ask the children to create a border for their screens including different knobs etc. Mount the television screens to create a display.

Reference to photocopiable sheet

The photocopiable page 147 shows a 1930s television set. There is space for children's own slogans.

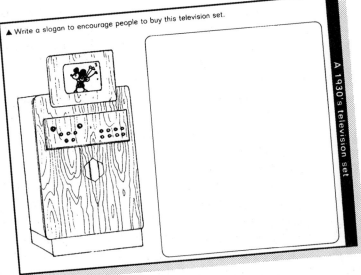

▲ Write a slogan to encourage people to buy this television set.

A 1930's television set

THE FIRST EMPEROR OF CHINA

To learn about the achievements of the first Emperor of China using different sources.

†† *Whole class then individuals working in groups.*

🕐 *Whole class 25 minutes; individuals variable.*

Previous skills/knowledge needed

This activity will draw on and extend children's awareness of how we find out about the past from different sources.

Key background information

Archaeological sources of information about Ancient China include details about the goods which were buried in tombs. Everything which the dead person needed for the afterlife was included: silk clothes; shoes; mirrors; bowls of food; models of servants and weapons. There are many written sources such as stories, prayers, household accounts, military orders and census returns to tell us about Ancient China. Buildings such as the Great Wall and other engineering feats such as the canals can still be seen today. Most of what we know about the First Emperor derives from archaeological sources and a history book called the *shiji*, written by Sima Qian, a hundred years after the time of the first emperor. Sima Qian didn't approve of all the things the first Emperor did and this needs to be taken into account when reading his history. According to the *shiji*, the First Emperor was born in 259 BC. He defeated several kingdoms which were fighting against each other and brought peace. In 221 BC he declared himself Emperor of China.

To control the empire and prevent wars from recurring the first Emperor created new laws and a system of harsh punishments. He sent his orders out in writing decreeing that this same writing was to be used throughout China. He introduced a standard coinage. The coins were bronze and circular with a square hole in the middle, so that they could be carried, threaded on to string. They were in use in China for the next 2000 years.

To protect the Empire, the Emperor built a Great Wall with watchtowers every few hundred metres. Soldiers used a variety of methods to contact each other, such as red and blue flags, fires at night and messages on strips of bamboo or wood (many of which have since been found).

Thousands of people were conscripted to build the Great Wall. The Emperor ordered a massive roadbuilding programme. During his reign, 4,250 miles (6,800km) were built, which was more than the total built during the Roman Empire. The roads enabled goods to be carried from place to place. Rice, pottery and silk were traded between cities and the Emperor became rich on the taxes which he levied. There were also many canals built during his reign, some of which are still in use today.

The First Emperor was terrified of dying and made elaborate plans for his after life. A gigantic tomb was made for him by 700,000 labourers who worked for 36 years. The historian Sima Qian reported that an entire palace was built underground. The roof was studded with jewels and whale oil lamps were designed to burn for eternity. The floor was made of precious metal in the shape of China and the rivers and lakes were made of mercury. The tomb was booby trapped with cross bows firing arrows against intruders. When the Emperor was buried his childless wives and many of the craftspeople who had made the tomb were killed and buried with him. The First Emperor's burial mound is 1,400 metres in circumference and 50 metres high. Archaeologists have not yet found the Emperor's actual burial chamber.

Buried close by, archaeologists have found over 6000 life-sized pottery soldiers guarding the Emperor's tomb, buried in different pits. The soldiers include infantry who were armed with bows, cross bows, swords, spears and dagger axes. There are charioteers with their guards who probably had long bamboo lances to prevent the enemy from chopping off the horses' heads. Cavalry soldiers were dressed in trousers and short tunics. None of the soldiers carried any shields since they were not expected to defend themselves but had to be always ready to attack. The soldiers are all different shapes and sizes and no two faces are alike. The Terracotta Army held real weapons, but some were stolen when grave robbers broke into the pits. Wooden crossbows have rotted away, but their bronze triggers remain.

The Terracotta Army
▲ Describe these terracotta soldiers. What clothes are they wearing? Do they have any weapons?

▲ Make a model of a terracotta soldier based on these designs.

Preparation
Prepare the photocopiable sheet on page 148 for each child to use as a source of information. It might be appropriate to stick the sheets on card and cover them with film to protect them. Prepare tables for working with clay and protective clothing for children.

Resources needed
Clay, modelling tools, clay boards, newspapers, pictures of China, Chinese writing, world map, photocopiable page 148.

What to do
Introduction
Locate China on a map of the world and talk about where it is in relation to the British Isles. Draw attention to the size of China in comparison with the British Isles. Refer to any available pictures of China to draw children's attention to the landscape. Look for any examples of Chinese writing and compare with scripts children are familiar with.
Development
Tell the children they are going to learn about the First Emperor of China. Talk with the children about the ways in which he united his Empire. Discuss the sources of evidence available to find out about the Emperor and his work.
Conclusion
Tell the children they are going to make some of the terracotta soldiers to guard the Emperor in his tomb. Hand out the photocopiable sheet for the children to look at. Talk about the clothes the soldiers wore and their armour. Organise one group at a time to make a soldier from clay. Ask the children to look closely at the details of the costume and to think

about the weapons which their soldier would be carrying. Some children might also like to model the horses which were found in the pits.

Suggestion(s) for extension

There are opportunities for children to research other aspects of Ancient China. For example some children might like to model the Great Wall of China with its watchtowers; other children could make replica coins to thread on string; some children could copy out some Chinese characters.

Suggestion(s) for support

This activity can be completed according to children's different abilities and stages of maturity.

Assessment opportunities

Can the children identify the different sources of evidence we can use to find out about the First Emperor? Can they suggest why some sources have been preserved and why others have been lost?

Opportunities for IT

Children could use a simple CD-ROM to research other information about China. They could be shown how to set up a simple search using keywords and how to browse the encyclopaedia using the highlighted words on the pages of information.

Display ideas

Position the model soldiers in rows to represent the soldiers standing in the great pit. Place roof timbers made from reclaimed materials above the soldiers and cover them with matting. A large mound to represent the Emperor's burial mound could be built close by. Children could paint a large frieze to provide a background for the Terracotta Army pit.

Reference to photocopiable sheet

The photocopiable page 148 shows some of the terracotta figures of the Chinese soldiers for the children to copy.

EMILY PANKHURST

To examine different views and attitudes of people in the past, and to learn about Emily Pankhurst.

†† *Whole class introduction; whole class development; individual.*

🕐 *20 minutes for each section.*

Previous skills/knowledge needed

This activity will draw on children's abilities to express their own points of view. Speaking and listening skills will be important.

Key background information

Emmeline Goulden was born in 1858 and married Dr Pankhurst in 1878. When he died, she took a job as registrar of births and deaths in a poor area of Manchester. It brought her into contact with great poverty and hardship. A working man's wage was hardly enough to support a family. Working class women also went out to work or took in work in their homes for very small wages. In addition these women would be expected to look after the home, cook and bring up the children. Due to increasing educational opportunities from the mid–nineteenth century onwards, more middle class

women were working particularly in secretarial, teaching, nursing and civil service jobs. However, this did not meet with approval with many people who thought a woman's place should be in the home and that it was 'unlady-like' to go out of the home to work. As middle class women became more educated, it seemed increasingly unfair that they should not have a say in the government of the country and opportunities to improve conditions and lives of women in all classes of society.

HISTORY KS1

In 1903 Mrs Pankhurst and her supporters founded the Women's Social and Political Union (WSPU) and began to campaign for female suffrage. Supporters regularly interrupted political meetings, they sought publicity and designed striking posters to get their message across. Big demonstrations and public rallies were held throughout the following years. Purple, white and green banners and flags were held aloft. A campaign of civil disobedience became increasingly violent: big demonstrations often ended in arrests and civil disorder, particularly if opponents of votes for women turned up for a fight; women threw stones and broke shop windows; there were several arson attacks; women chained themselves to street railings and refused to move.

Many women were imprisoned. Once inside the prison many refused to eat and the government was forced to release them. Prison staff tried various tactics against the hunger strikers; tempting food was provided to persuade them to eat; sometimes they were put in solitary confinement and some were made to wear handcuffs. Some hunger strikers were force fed. This meant holding them down whilst food was poured down a tube which was stuck down their throat. In 1913 the first death amongst the suffragettes occurred when Emily Davison threw herself under the king's horse, during the Derby at Epsom. She died in hospital a few days later.

When the First World War began in 1914, suffragettes supported the war effort; women took over many jobs formerly done by men and encouraged the men to go and fight. In many industries, women earned much less than men doing the same work. In 1917 the government at last introduced a bill to give women the vote. It was still opposed by many; for example, Lord Curzon in the House of Lords said that it would be the ruin of Britain. Women over the age of 30 were granted the vote when it became law in 1918.

Men could vote at the age of 21. If all women over 21 had been able to vote they would have outnumbered the men! All women over 21 were finally given the vote in 1928. In the 1918 election, 17 women stood as candidates, but none were successful. The first female MP was Lady Astor who was elected as the representative for Plymouth in 1919.

Preparation

Cut up enough coloured cards to give to about half the class. Make a posting box similar to a black ballot box. Prepare the photocopiable sheet on page 149 for each child.

Resources needed

Pictures of everyday scenes, including suffragettes, between 1900–1920. Coloured cards, ballot box, photocopiable sheet on page 149, pencils, crayons, felt-tipped pens.

What to do

Introduction

Hand out coloured cards to half of the children in the class. You might choose just to give them to all the boys or to children at random. Tell the children that they are going to be asked their opinion on some aspect of the running of the school or their classroom. Topics which could be included are designing the playground with new play equipment; discussing new resources which could be bought for the classroom; making a list of rules for behaviour in school; re-designing the book corner/library to encourage readers. Tell the children if they want to contribute any ideas they must hold up the card which they have been given at the beginning of the lesson. Ignore children who put up their hands, but do not hold a card. When the discussion has finished the cards can be posted in a ballot box.

Development

Remind the children about the earlier discussion and ask the children who did not have a card how they felt to be excluded from the discussion and decision-making. Cardholders might also like to contribute their views. Tell the children that a similar occasion occurred nearly 100 years ago, when women were not permitted to make their opinions heard or to vote for Members of Parliament. You will need to explain some of the work of Parliament in passing laws which effect people's lives. Children might be familiar with some laws which affect their own lives for example seat belt laws; school attendance laws; film classifications.

Provide the children with information about what it must have been like for women at the turn of the century. Explain how Mrs Pankhurst wanted to improve the lives of women and wanted women's views to be taken into account. Talk about the campaign of civil disobedience. Ask the children if they think the suffragettes were right to disobey the law. What action would they have taken? You might like to draw children's attention to ways in which people try to influence politicians and the media today. They might have heard of protest meetings, marches and demonstrations or seen them on the television.

Conclusion

Hand out the photocopiable sheet to each child. Ask the children to think of reasons why Mrs Pankhurst wanted to vote; what sort of things might she say in her speech? Ask the children to fill in the words which Mrs Pankhurst is saying in the speech bubble on the sheet. The picture can be coloured in and the appropriate colours used for the suffragette banners.

Suggestion(s) for extension

Children could think of reasons why women should not be allowed to vote. They might like to draw a character, dressed in appropriate costume putting an opposing viewpoint in a speech bubble. Children could try to design their own poster to persuade the government to give them the vote.

Suggestion(s) for support

Some children might find difficulty writing in the speech bubble. They could be encouraged to write the slogan, 'Votes for Women'.

Assessment opportunities

Can the children put forward views on the fairness of male only suffrage? Are the children able to describe any of the reasons why women wanted the vote?

Opportunities for IT

Children could use specific software which enables them to make large paper banners to design and print out their own suffragette banners for display in the classroom.

Older or more able pupils might be able to work as a group and use a word processor to write a short speech to persuade the government to give women voting rights. They could use the same approach to a more personal or immediate issue related to home or school, for example keeping the playground clean; having longer playtimes; or staying up to see a television programme.

Display ideas

Create a large scene of a suffrage rally. Children can research costume worn at the time and draw and colour different people standing in the crowd. They will need to include policemen too. Mrs Pankhurst can be placed on a raised platform talking to the crowd.

Reference to photocopiable sheet

The photocopiable page 149 shows Mrs Pankhurst standing beneath a Suffragette banner giving a speech. Children can complete what she is saying by filling in the space in the speech bubble.

Past events and celebrations

The activities in this section relate to past events of various types. Information is provided about a range of events which include national events which have been remembered and commemorated by succeeding generations, religious festivals and different celebrations. These events have been drawn from different historical periods and cultural traditions. The activities provide opportunities for class, individual and group work.

Many of the activities are introduced through stories to introduce children to aspects of ways of life in the past, including different values and attitudes. Children are encouraged to reflect on why certain events occurred and the effects of such events on daily life and the course of history. The activities introduce children to particular historical sources of information including artefacts, pictures and photographs, adults talking about the past, written sources and buildings and sites. Different ways in which the past has been represented and is commemorated is explored in some of the activities. Children are invited to make some of their own representations of the past. Suggestions to stimulate children's historical enquiry and questioning skills are included. Children are encouraged to demonstrate their historical knowledge and understanding in a variety of ways including written accounts, paintings and drawings, model making and role-play activities.

AROUND THE YEAR

To develop children's experience of seasonal change and to provide opportunities to use words and phrases relating to the passing of time.

†† *Whole class; pairs.*

⊕ *Whole class; 20 minutes; pairs 25 minutes; whole class ongoing.*

Previous skills/knowledge needed

This activity can develop from any other work on seasons of the year.

Key background information

This activity provides opportunities for the children to talk about the passage of time and to note the changes which occur throughout the year.

Preparation

Organise a collection of different pictures and artefacts which relate to the different seasons. Prepare the photocopiable sheet on page 150 per pair of children.

Resources needed

Books and pictures depicting different times of the year. Articles of clothing which can be worn at different times. Collection of different celebration cards for example Christmas; Easter; Diwali; Eid. Pencils, colouring materials, scissors. Photocopiable sheet on page 150.

Changes through the seasons
▲ Draw pictures to show what happens in the different seasons

What to do

Introduction

Begin by talking about the current season of the year. What is the weather like? What activities do the children enjoy doing? Talk about the clothes they are wearing. Talk about the plants and trees outside and animal life. Match some of the pictures, cards and artefacts from the resources to the season you have been discussing.

Select some resources for a contrasting season and encourage the children to talk about some of the differences with the current season. How do the seasons affect our lives, and the lives of plants and animals? Talk about the other seasons and encourage the children to be aware of some of the differences.

Development

Tell the children they are going to draw some seasonal pictures to show some of the differences which occur during the year. Pair the children and ask them to select two different seasons each. Hand out the photocopiable sheet and encourage the children to discuss with each other the things they are going to draw in their pictures. Maybe they could use the pictures to tell a story of different children, plants and animals at particular times of the year.

Conclusion

When the pictures are finished, ask the children to cut them out and to exchange them with another pair of children. Can they place the pictures in the correct order and explain why they have chosen their particular sequence? Re-assemble the children and sequence some of the pictures together as a class. Create opportunities for the children to become familiar with time vocabulary: before; after; next; then; first; second and the names of the seasons.

Suggestion(s) for extension

Children may like to make their own season book where they can draw and write about the different seasons.

Suggestion(s) for support

Some children may need prompting to discuss factors about the seasons and will need practice with time vocabulary. The photocopiable sheet could be used for the children to draw a picture of the current season. Then at a later date they could be invited to draw another picture and continue to build up their seasons as the year passes, rather than drawing all the pictures at the same time.

Assessment opportunities

Listen to the children talking about their pictures. Are they familiar with some vocabulary of time? Can they recognise some of the changes occurring in different seasons?

Opportunities for IT

Children could use a word processor to write simple sentences about the various seasons. This could be done as a group activity with each member of the group writing their own line or sentence about the season, these could then be printed out for display in the classroom.

Children could also use an art package to draw a seasonal picture or pattern based on a colour, such as green for spring or brown for autumn. If the art package allowed it they could experiment by mixing different shades of the base colour.

Display ideas

Display a collection of seasonal objects and provide labels to reinforce children's language and time vocabulary. Cut out a large circle and divide it into quarters. Label each quarter a particular season and ask the children to stick their pictures in the appropriate place. Make a pointer which can be attached to the centre and which can be moved to point to the different seasons as they occur.

Reference to photocopiable sheet

The photocopiable page 150 has spaces for four pictures. The children are asked in pairs to draw a picture representing each of the four seasons.

THE CHINESE CALENDAR

To extend children's knowledge of how time has been recorded in different cultures and to learn about New Year celebrations and traditions.

†† *Whole class; individual.*

🕐 *Whole class 25 minutes; individual 20 minutes.*

Previous skills/knowledge needed

This activity will extend children's experiences of the calendar and the measurement of the passage of time.

Key background information

The Chinese calendar follows a twelve-year cycle which has remained unchanged for two thousand years since the Han dynasty. Each year is named after an animal which has certain characteristics attributed to it. The New Year festival is based

on the lunar calendar and usually occurs in late January or early February. Traditionally New Year's Day was followed by 15 days of celebrations, but now it is more usual to celebrate for three days: New Year's Eve, New Year's Day and Kai Nien, the following day. A special dinner is held on New Year's Eve and everybody is encouraged to stay up to welcome the New Year in. New Year's Day is a fast day. New clothes are worn and children are given lucky red money envelopes called *lai see*. On Kai Nien (the day following New Year's Day) a special meal is eaten with friends and family.

There are several versions on how the years were named after the animals. One version relates how all the animals were arguing about who would give their name to the first year so loudly that they woke up the gods. The gods suggested that the animals should have a race and the New Year would be named after the winner. The ox was winning, but as he was swimming across the river the rat jumped onto his nose and leapt ashore to win the race. Consequently the New Year cycle always begins with the rat and is followed by  the ox and the other animals in the order in which they finished the race: tiger; rabbit; dragon; snake; horse; sheep; monkey; rooster; dog; pig. 1996 is the Year of the Rat, 1997 the Year of the Ox and so on.

Preparation

Prepare the photocopiable sheet on page 151 for pairs of children to share. Set out painting materials and paper on a painting table.

Resources needed

Pictures showing Chinese celebrations of the New Year. Photocopiable sheet on page 151. Large piece of paper, pencils, painting materials.

What to do

Introduction

Discuss with the children important occasions which occur during the year, for example birthdays, religious festivals, anniversaries. Talk about how they are celebrated. Are any special foods eaten or special clothes worn? Do people give or receive presents? Are decorations put up?

Development

Use the background information to tell the children how the Chinese New Year is celebrated. Refer to any pictures about the celebrations from your resources if they are available. Tell the story about how the years acquired their names. As the names of the different animals are mentioned ask the children to consider the movements of the different animals. Children might like to act out the different ways the animals moved to try and win the race. Include in the story the different

landscapes which the animals raced through, there were mountains, jungles, deserts. Explain how the rat finally won the race.

Hand out the photocopiable sheet and talk about the different animals. Find out the name of the current Chinese Year and locate this animal on the sheet. Can the children work out what next year will be called? What was last year called? Can the children work out the name of the year when they were born? Use the sheet to provide opportunities for children to develop their historical vocabulary for example to talk about before, after and next.

Conclusion
Ask the children to select one of the animals and to draw and paint a picture of it to contribute to a class display depicting the race.

Suggestion(s) for extension
Ask the children to write down the dates of the years of the different animals. For example: '1996 is the Year of the Rat'.

Children can find out the birth years of other members of their family and work out which year they were born in using the photocopiable sheet. Children can research the different characteristics attached to people born in different years.

Suggestion(s) for support
Some children may need extra time to discuss the calendar work. Encourage them to act out the various animals to help their understanding of the story.

Assessment opportunities
What experiences do children describe in talking about celebrations in their lives? Do they know why different celebrations are held?

Opportunities for IT
Children could create a simple database of festivals giving a range of simple data which might include:

Festival	Christmas
Religion	Christianity
Time of year	winter
Dates	25th December
Reason	celebrates the birth of Jesus
Description	giving of presents, parties, decorations

The *description* filed might include a brief account of what happens in the festivals or what the festival celebrates. This might not be possible with all databases as it may only be possible to enter a single word. Other types of databases may have a free text file where it is possible to write as much or as little as you want.

Once the database has been created children could search to find the most common time of the year for festivals, or different religions.

Display ideas
Create a large frieze using the painted animals running the race. The frieze can be labelled with key 'time' words, for example first, last, next, before. Children might also like to make models of the different animals using Plasticine or clay.

Make dragons to celebrate the New Year. Take two strips of coloured paper, (red, gold, green) 70–80cm long and 4–5cms wide. Staple the papers together at one end and fold the paper in zigzags over each other. Draw a dragon's head on another piece of paper and attach it to the last zigzag. Add eyes to make the dragon come alive. Strips of thin card can be added to the head and tail to make the dragon dance.

Reference to photocopiable sheet
The photocopiable sheet on page 151 shows the cycle of the Chinese Years.

New Year race

THE BATTLE OF HASTINGS

To find out about the Battle of Hastings from a range of sources of information. To sequence events, in order to develop a sense of chronology.

†† *Whole class, then pairs/individuals*

🕐 *Whole class 20 minutes; pairs/individuals 25 minutes.*

Previous skills/knowledge needed

This activity requires familiarity with story sequencing skills and involves some reading. Cutting and pasting skills.

Key background information

We know a great deal about the events leading up to the battle of Hastings from the Bayeux tapestry and accounts written by French and English chroniclers. These sources provide different versions of the background to the battle and of the battle itself. The account from the Bayeux tapestry is included on the photocopiable sheet. The Bayeux tapestry is really an embroidery with the figures sewn, not woven on the material. It measures just over 70 metres long and half a metre wide and is on display in Bayeux, Normandy. Various features suggest that the tapestry was probably made during the decade following the battle of Hastings. It is thought to have been commissioned by Bishop Odo, William's half brother, and presents the Norman view of 1066 and the events which led up to the battle of Hastings.

The story of the Battle of Hastings

▲ Connect the sentences to the pictures. They will tell you the story of the battle of Hastings.

- Harold is killed
- William sets sail
- Harold the King
- The ships are loaded with weapons and armour
- William leads his men into battle

▲ Add your own sentence and picture on a separate piece of paper.

The King of England, Edward the Confessor, died without children and was succeeded by Harold Godwinson, the powerful Earl of Wessex. William, Duke of Normandy, also had claims to the English throne and argued that Edward had named him as his successor. Moreover, William claimed that Harold too, had supported him. The Bayeux tapestry shows that before Edward died Harold took an oath on some holy relics promising to help William. Edward the Confessor died on January 5th 1066 and was buried in the newly consecrated Westminster Abbey. When William heard that Harold had become king, he immediately planned to invade England. The Bayeux tapestry shows the ships being built and loaded with stores; coats of chain mail, arrows and other weapons and barrels of wine. The Bayeux tapestry shows William and his soldiers celebrating their arrival at Pevensey Bay with a feast and by building a wooden fort. In the meantime, King Harold was far away in the north of England, fighting off an attack launched by the king of Norway in conjunction with King Harold's brother, Tostig. King Harold fought a decisive battle at Stamford Bridge, near York, on the 25th September, and then on hearing news of William's invasion had to begin the long march to Hastings. Harold and his men were exhausted when they reached the vicinity of Hastings. They camped on the ridge of a hill and prepared for battle. The English troops massed together behind a deep shield wall. The following morning, the battle began with the Norman archers firing their arrows ineffectually against the shields. The Norman cavalry attacked and there was a great deal of hand-to-hand fighting. The two sides were evenly matched. During the battle, William fell from his horse and the Bayeux tapestry depicts him raising his helmet as a signal that he was safe. Towards evening, when both sides were almost exhausted, William instructed his archers to fire their arrows high into the air, above the wall of shields. The arrows inflicted heavy casualties on the English, weakening them considerably. King Harold was killed. The Bayeux tapestry shows a soldier trying to remove an arrow from his own eye, traditionally assumed to be Harold. More recent research suggests that Harold was hacked to pieces by four Norman knights. Harold's death was decisive; his men lost heart and William won the battle. William then marched on to London and on Christmas Day 1066, was crowned King in Westminster Abbey.

Preparation

Prepare the photocopiable sheet on page 152 for each child or pairs of children.

Resources needed

Pictures and books of the battle of Hastings and the Bayeux tapestry. Scissors. Adhesive. Strips of card. Crayons and felt-tipped pens. Photocopiable page 152.

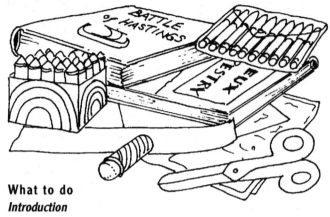

What to do

Introduction

Talk about the royal family. What happens when a monarch dies? Who succeeds to the throne? What is a coronation? Talk about the different symbols of monarchy; the orb, sceptre and crown.

Development

Present the children with the problem that Edward the Confessor was dying and had no children as heirs. Can the children suggest any solutions? Re-tell the story of the battle of Hastings using the background information. Ask the children if they think William was right to invade England to seize the crown. What do they think the people in England might have thought about William? Use the story to provide children with background information about life at the time and include details about the soldiers' weapons and armour. Talk about the different sources of information available which tell us about what happened in 1066.

Conclusion

Hand out the photocopiable sheets and explain that the pictures are copies from the Bayeux tapestry, which is one source of information. Talk about what the children can see in the pictures. Ask the children to cut out the pictures and to arrange them in the correct sequence and to write out the labels, placing them under the appropriate picture. Children can add their own picture and writing. They might like to refer to additional books and pictures from your resources. The pictures and writing can be pasted onto a strip of card to tell the story of the battle of Hastings.

Suggestion(s) for extension

Children can add more pictures to their Bayeux strip and write more about the story of the battle of Hastings. Children could investigate the ships which crossed the Channel and shipbuilding techniques, page 68.

Suggestion(s) for support

Pair children needing support with more able readers and encourage them to talk about their sequence. Limit the number of pictures for the children to sequence. Ask them to select a picture which shows the beginning and the end of the story.

Assessment opportunities

Can the children sequence the story in the correct order? Can the children use the Bayeux tapestry to talk about different aspects of life in the eleventh century?

Opportunities for IT

Children might be able to use an encyclopaedia CD-ROM to look up information about the Norman Conquest. There is also a separate CD-ROM which deals specifically with the Bayeux Tapestry.

Children could also use an art package to create their own version of the Bayeux Tapestry. If they work in pairs, each pair could sketch out a design for their picture and then use the art package to draw and colour it. Each part could be printed out and the whole Tapestry mounted together. The class could decide how many different sections would be needed if they are to work in pairs, and then what each section should be about.

Of course this work does not have to be the Norman Conquest, it could be a more modern event, such as the first man to land on the moon (see page 108).

Display ideas

Select a scene from the Bayeux tapestry and create a large collage. Children can draw, paint or sew their own figures onto the scene.

Reference to the photocopiable sheet

The photocopiable page 152 shows different scenes taken from the Bayeux tapestry. In their correct order, the first picture depicts Harold as he is crowned king. He is holding the orb and sceptre and the archbishop is by his side. The second picture shows coats of chain mail and a variety of weapons being taken to the ships. A cart laden with a barrel of wine and arrows is being pulled along. There follows the

picture of the ships setting sail with the Norman soldiers and their horses. The fourth picture shows the beginning of the battle with the Norman archers and cavalry attacking the English. In the final picture, it is widely thought that Harold is the figure on the extreme right hand side. It is believed that he has been ridden-down by a Norman horseman and has let his long battle axe drop.

THE MAYFLOWER AND HARVEST CELEBRATIONS IN THE UNITED STATES

To learn about the Pilgrim Fathers and how their journey and settlement in America has been commemorated by succeeding generations. To learn about aspects of life in the seventeenth century through the story.

†† *Whole class and individuals.*

🕐 *Whole class 20 minutes; individuals 15 minutes.*

Previous skills/knowledge needed
Some awareness of the importance of the harvest for survival would be helpful. This activity could develop from 'Growing Corn', page 63.

Key background information
The Pilgrim Fathers were Puritans; people who preferred a simple life with strict religious observances. They disliked the ceremony of the Church of England, but were not allowed to practise their Puritan faith under King James I and so sought new lands where they could worship as they pleased. *The Mayflower* was a small ship (about 25 metres long and 7 metres broad at her widest), which sailed from Southampton in 1620 with her sister ship *The Speedwell*.

The Speedwell sprung a leak so both ships stopped off at Plymouth where *The Speedwell's* passengers transferred to *The Mayflower* which then set off with 101 passengers and 20–30 crew members.

The Mayflower's hold was packed with tools, weapons, fishing equipment, ropes, blankets, clothing, barrels of gunpowder and all sorts of provisions such as dried peas, salt meat, flour, grain and hard biscuits. The conditions on the crossing were difficult; food supplies ran low and the passengers were reduced to eating rats. The Pilgrims sang psalms and hymns to keep their spirits up. A great storm blew up which cracked one of the main beams. The high seas crashed against the deck and the passengers all huddled below decks. One man was washed overboard by a giant wave and then washed back again. Surprisingly only one man died during the journey and was buried at sea. A baby was born on the voyage too!

After 65 days the Pilgrims finally reached Massachusetts in North America. They called their new home Plymouth. They were very weak but had to begin building shelters. They began to make friends with native Americans and with their help set about planting their seed for the following harvest. They planted peas and barley. The native Americans taught them how to plant maize and how to use herrings as manure. They also taught them how to make maple syrup and how to trap animals for their fur. By the end of the first year half of the pilgrims had died. The remaining settlers organised a thanksgiving feast to celebrate the harvest and to thank God for their settlement. North Americans still celebrate Thanksgiving Day in November each year to commemorate the bravery of the first European settlers. Turkey and pumpkin pie are traditionally served on this day.

Preparation
Prepare the photocopiable sheet on page 153 sufficient for each child to work independently.

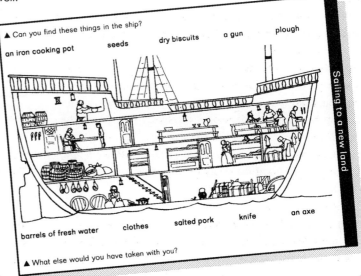

▲ Can you find these things in the ship?

an iron cooking pot seeds dry biscuits a gun plough

barrels of fresh water clothes salted pork knife an axe

▲ What else would you have taken with you?

Sailing to a new land

105

Resources needed

Some props to help tell the story, for example some dried peas and barley; a map of the Atlantic; pictures of seventeenth-century ships; an old cooking pot, photocopiable sheet on page 153, pencils and colouring materials.

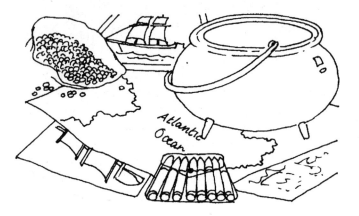

What to do

Discuss with the children different reasons for moving home. This can be a sensitive issue and will need handling with care. Explain that the children are going to learn about people who moved home and crossed to America to build their new homes. Using the background information tell the story of the Pilgrim Fathers. Refer to some of the props in the resources to stimulate children's interest in the story. Provide opportunities for the children to relate the story to some of their more familiar experiences.

What sort of things would the children take with them if they were moving house? Talk about going on a long journey. What food would the children take with them? Compare their ideas with the things taken by the Pilgrim Fathers. Talk about the dangers of the voyage and the hard work which the first settlers undertook to build their first settlement. Tell the children about the Thanksgiving feast. Do the children think it is a good way to commemorate the Pilgrim Fathers?

Hand out the photocopiable sheet and ask the children to find the different objects hidden in the ships. They can circle the objects which they have found on the sheet. Can the children explain why each of these objects was needed?

Suggestion(s) for extension

Children can write their own log of the voyage. They could include incidents such as the storm and running out of food. Encourage them to write about how they felt during their voyage and on their arrival in America.

Use an atlas or globe for children to locate Southampton in England and trace the route of the voyage to Plymouth, Massachusetts in North America.

Suggestion(s) for support

Children might need help matching the words with pictures on the photocopiable sheet. They could draw other things which the Pilgrims would need.

Assessment opportunities

Can the children explain why the Pilgrims needed the different objects for their voyage? Note the comments which children make about life in the seventeenth century.

Opportunities for IT

Children could use a CD-ROM to look for information about the Pilgrim Fathers.

Children could also write their own *Mayflower* diary using a word processor. This would involve them in saving and retrieving the text so that they could add to it at a later date. Different groups of children could write from different perspectives for example: a child, the captain of the ship, one of the pilgrim fathers.

Display ideas

Create life below decks in the play area. The living conditions were very cramped. Passengers slept on straw mattresses. Cooking fires were lit in a box of sand. Provide a lantern and some cooking and eating utensils. A chart of the Atlantic Ocean and a telescope would provide opportunities for children to navigate to North America. Rope for fishing and tying things together would be useful. Clothes could include white bonnets and tall black hats, breeches, long skirts and shoes with buckles. Encourage the children to suggest other items which they think they would need.

Reference to photocopiable sheet

The photocopiable page 153 shows some of the objects which the Pilgrim Fathers took on their voyage: a plough; an axe; an iron cooking pot; a knife; barrels of fresh water; a gun; dry biscuits; salted pork; seeds; clothes.

THE GREAT FIRE OF LONDON

To learn about the Great Fire of London from different sources.

†† *Whole class; individuals.*

⏱ *Whole class 20 minutes; individuals variable.*

Previous skills/knowledge needed

Some experience of writing diaries would be helpful.

Key background information

The Fire of London started on the 2 September 1666, in a baker's shop in Pudding Lane. The old houses were timber framed with thatched roofs and were built close to each other so that the fire moved on from one house to the next quite rapidly. Attempts to extinguish the fire were made with people running to gather water in leather buckets from the Thames.

The wind blew strongly and the fire took hold. Many people fled, taking with them what belongings they could across the Thames to the other side of the river. The wind continued to blow strongly and the buckets and syringes of water were not enough to extinguish the flames. Near the centre of the fire it was very hot; lead dripped off the roofs of the churches and the stained glass cracked with the heat. It seemed as if nothing would stop the fire and so the decision was made to blow up the houses in the path of the fire so that the fire would have nothing to burn. Gunpowder was used and King Charles himself supervised some of the work.

The Great Fire lasted for four days and nights. On the third day the strong wind suddenly dropped and the fire gradually died down. Half the city had been destroyed. Thirteen thousand homes, 84 churches and many other buildings had been burned to the ground. Over 100,000 people were made homeless. Plans were drawn up for re-building the city with wider streets and buildings of brick or stone. St Paul's cathedral had been burned to the ground and a new cathedral was designed to replace it by Sir Christopher Wren. The story of the fire is written in the diaries of Samuel Pepys and John Evelyn and there are several pictures and drawings of the fire. Archaeologists have also found pieces of charred wood from the burned houses.

Preparation

Prepare the photocopiable sheet on page 154 for each child.

Resources needed

Pictures and books of the Fire of London. Photocopiable sheet on page 154, pencils and writing materials.

What to do

Introduction

Begin by singing with the children the rhyme, *London's Burning*, and explain to the children they are going to learn about a great fire in London. Use the background information

to tell them the story of the Great Fire. Ask the children to think of reasons why the fire burned so long. How do we know so much about the fire? Discuss the different sources of evidence we have about the fire. Hand out photocopiable sheet on page 154, children will probably need help reading the extracts. What did Pepys do during the fire? Talk about the things which Pepys recorded in his diary.

Development

Encourage the children to take on the role of someone at the fire, such as: the baker in Pudding Lane; the owner of a boat ferrying people across the Thames; someone with a home in the path of the fire. Think about what they might have done during the fire. Would they have helped? Would they have tried to escape? What would they have done with their valuable possessions? Encourage the children to describe the scene of the fire; what could they see and what did London look like when the fire was finally extinguished?

Conclusion

Ask the children to make their own diary of the fire by writing or drawing their own version of the events. Begin with an entry for 2 September 1666.

Suggestion(s) for extension

Encourage the children to research more about Samuel Pepys and what happened to London after the Great Fire.

Suggestion(s) for support

Children who find writing difficult might like to draw a sequence of the events of the Great Fire. Alternatively they might draw one picture to represent the story.

Assessment opportunities
Can the children talk about some of the sources of information about the Great Fire? Can they explain how we know what happened?

Opportunities for IT
Different groups of children could write their own account of the Great Fire considering different viewpoints and using a word processor.

Children could also use an art package to draw their own version of the fire, experimenting with different shapes and colours for the flames.

Display ideas
Create a large collage to depict the fire. Make a dark background with silhouettes of buildings, including Old St Paul's Cathedral and London Bridge. Use orange, red and yellow paper cut in the shape of flames to show flames emerging from the windows and buildings of the silhouettes. Display some of the diary extracts written by the children around the collage.

Reference to photocopiable sheet
The photocopiable sheet on page 154 has excerpts from the diary written by Samuel Pepys during the Fire of London. The second half and the reverse side of the sheet provides space for the children to write/draw their own diary entries.

THE FIRST MOON LANDING

To learn about the first landing on the Moon drawing on a range of different sources for information.
†† *Whole class, groups of four children.*
🕐 *Whole class 15 minutes; groups variable.*

Previous skills/knowledge needed
This activity will draw on children's model-building skills.

Key background information
The race for the first landing on the moon really took off in the 1950s. In 1957 the Russians sent a dog called Laika into space in *Sputnik 2*. In 1961 Yuri Gagarin made the first space flight in the rocket called *Vostok*. The first space walk was made by Alexei Leonov in 1965. The Americans were the first to land on the moon in July 1969. This was an event watched on television screens all over the world; 'living history'. The *Apollo 11* spacecraft took off on July 16th with Neil Armstrong, Edwin Aldrin and Michael Collins on board. Four days later, Neil Armstrong and Edwin Aldrin separated from the spacecraft and landed on the moon in a lunar

module. Armstrong was the first man to step on the moon, with the words, ' That's one small step for a man, one giant leap for mankind.'. Samples of lunar rock and dust were collected to take back to earth and various pieces of equipment were set up before the lunar module set off to join the spacecraft orbiting the moon. Aldrin and Armstrong transferred to Apollo 11 which set off to return to earth and a final splash-down in the Pacific Ocean. The footprints of the astronauts remain on the surface of the moon, since there is no wind or water there. The astronauts' spacesuits were vital for the mission. They were needed to keep the astronauts warm, protect them against harmful rays, supply oxygen for them to breathe and to surround their bodies with pressurised atmosphere. Space suits are bulky and difficult to walk in. They are made up of many different layers with a shiny top layer. The suit would be heavy to wear on earth, but in space with no gravity it doesn't feel heavy.

Preparation
Ask children to gather different sorts of information about space travel. They can ask members of their families what they remember of the first moon landing. Have they any souvenirs or mementoes of the event? Make a moon base from a large flat surface. Crumple up newspaper to represent the moon's craters. Paint over the newspaper using thick grey and white paints. Sprinkle some powder paint to give the effect of dust. Some parts could be covered with a layer of bright orange dust.

Resources needed
Pictures and books of space travel. Pictures of the earth from space. Card, scissors, adhesive, pencils, crayons, felt-tipped pens, construction and reclaimed materials.

What to do
Introduction
Look at some of the pictures of space ships and space travel. Using the background information, talk to the children about the race to land the first person on the moon and the moon

landing in July 1969. Discuss the special equipment astronauts take with them into space, their clothing and food. This activity enables children to draw on a wide range of sources. Ask the children how we know so much information about the first moon landing. Encourage them to think about different sources, for example television; photographs; the conversations and accounts of the astronauts; memories of people living at the time; souvenirs made to commemorate the event.

Development
Tell the children they are going to make a model of the first moon landing. Talk about things that they will need to include, for example astronauts; lunar module; flag. Help children to identify the different tasks which need to be done to complete the model.

Conclusion
Children can be encouraged to use a variety of materials for their models. Encourage them to look closely at pictures for details of the astronauts' clothing and the lunar module and to try and copy them in their model making. When the models are completed place them on a model of the moon's surface to record the first moon landing.

Suggestion(s) for extension
Encourage children to find out more about space exploration and to record their information in either a class or individual space book. Children can contribute towards a space timeline illustrating the chief events in space exploration.

Suggestion(s) for support
Some children may need help with cutting and pasting. The activity is such that it provides opportunities for all children to respond according to their different abilities and various stages of development.

Assessment opportunities
What sources of information do the children suggest can be used for finding out about space travel?

Opportunities for IT
Children could use a CD-ROM to look for information about the different space flights. There are some CD-ROMs which are dedicated to just this and provide text and pictures as well as sounds.

Use a word processor for the children to keep a diary of the different days on the trip to the moon. They may need to save their work so that it can be retrieved later and new entries added or previous ones amended. Children could also keep this diary using a tape recorder, rewinding the recorder to the start of the entry, or editing it.

Make labels for a space timeline using the word processor and these can then be displayed in the classroom. Each pair of children could research and write about one important event. They could type in their own text and then decide which font to use and how to make the print so that it is easy to read the label.

Children could also use a *Roamer* or floor turtle and pretend that they are directing a lunar vehicle from earth. They could make their own lunar landscape for the *Roamer* to explore. If some obstacles such as a crater or hill are added the children can practise directing the *Roamer* around the area to visit certain features, or go around the edge of the crater. This will give them an opportunity to practise giving accurate and precise commands.

Display ideas
Children can investigate the interiors of different space craft and make their own spacecraft in the classroom play area. Encourage them to make different computer screens, switchboards and navigational equipment from reclaimed materials and to attach knobs and dials. Provide charts of the universe for children to select their destinations, and log books for them to record their journeys.

HISTORY KS1

THE OLYMPIC GAMES

To learn about a past event from a different culture.
To find out about aspects of the past from a range of sources.

†† *Whole class then individuals or pairs.*

🕐 *Whole class 20 minutes; individuals/pairs 25 minutes.*

Previous skills/knowledge needed
This activity requires careful cutting skills.

Key background information
The original Olympic games were first held around 776 BC and ended around AD 396. They took place every four years in midsummer and were a religious festival as well as an athletic one. A few weeks before they were opened, messengers would travel around the various Greek communities proclaiming a sacred truce and inviting competitors and spectators to come to the festival. During the festival all communities were expected to be at peace with one another and under the protection of Zeus, 'father of gods and men'. Athletic competitions took place in the stadium and chariot racing in the hippodrome. There were running events over different distances, including one race when competitors wore armour. The pentathlon comprised five events: jumping; discus; javelin; a foot race over a short distance; wrestling. Victors were awarded olive crowns, cut from the sacred olive tree, which stood behind the temple of Zeus. Other communities also held great games festivals in honour of other gods. Various sources provide us with

information about the games, for example archaeological sites; pottery (Greek vase painters included scenes from athletics); sculpture; literature. The modern Olympic games were first held in Athens in 1896 and are now held every four years in different countries. The Olympic flame is lit in Greece and runners carry it all the way to the place where the games are to be held.

Preparation
Duplicate the required number of copies of photocopiable sheets page 155 (one per child or pair of children).

Resources needed
Books and pictures about Ancient Greece. Information about the modern Olympics such as newspaper reports and photographs. Photocopiable page 155, adhesive, scissors, pieces of card/paper, orange and black crayons.

What to do.
Introduction
Ask the children what sporting events they know about. Perhaps some children have attended sports matches or games, watched them on the television or seen pictures of them in the newspaper? Talk about athletics and the different track and field events, for example running, discus, long jump and javelin. Tell the children about the Olympic games today. Talk about the games which are organised and how competitors come from all over the world to compete for gold, silver and bronze medals. Explain how athletes train hard to be selected to represent their country at the Olympic games, which are held every four years. The games are opened with a procession of competitors marching through the arena, and the Olympic flame is lit. Explain how we can gain information about the present Olympics from the television and you could look together at some newspaper reports/pictures in books.
Development
Explain to the children how the present Olympic games have developed from games held a very long time ago in a Greek city called Olympia. Use the background information to tell the children about the Ancient Greek games.

The Ancient Greek games

Conclusion

Use the background information to talk about the different sources of information which tell us about the Games. Show the children some pictures of Ancient Greek buildings and sites and of some pots to demonstrate the sort of sources that are available. Explain to the children that often the sources are found in different fragments and archaeologists have to put together the different pieces to try and obtain a complete picture.

Tell the children they are going to work as archaeologists. A pot has been found but unfortunately it has been broken into pieces. Working as archaeologists the children will have to try and fit all the pieces together and see if the pot can provide any useful information about the Olympic games. Hand out the photocopiable sheet. Ask the children to cut around the different pieces of pot and to try and stick them together on card to recreate a whole pot. What event in the games is illustrated on the pot? The children can colour in their re-constructed pot using black and orange crayons.

Suggestion(s) for extension

Ask the children to look at books and pictures about Ancient Greece and to draw or make a list of different sources of information which would tell them about life at that time. Can the children find any more information about Ancient Greek games from pots and different archaeological sites?

Organise your own Olympic games. Divide the children into different groups to be athletes representing different Greek towns and cities, for example Athens, Corinth, Sparta, Delphi, Epidaurus. Organise different Olympic events such as running races, jumping. Some games can be adapted for example replace the discus with a small hoop, ball or beanbag.

Suggestion(s) for support

Children might find difficulty cutting out the different pieces and will need help sticking them together. Some children might find working in pairs helpful for this activity.

Assessment opportunities

Can the children respond to the question: how do we know about the Ancient Greek Olympics? Can they suggest some of the sources which provide information? For example pots, sites and writing.

Display ideas

Create a display of Greek pots. Cut out the shapes of different pots in orange sugar paper. Ask the children to draw and colour in black the competitors taking part in one of the events at the Olympic games. Encourage them to look carefully at Ancient Greek pots, trying to copy some of the patterns to decorate the top and bottom of their pot.

Reference to photocopiable sheet

The photocopiable page 155 shows fragments of an Ancient Greek pot with a picture of runners in a race.

THE EISTEDDFOD AND THE GORSEDD OF THE BARDS

To learn about an event which has been commemorated for many years, and how and why some of the ceremonies originated.

†† *Whole class; individual.*

🕐 *Whole class introduction variable; development 20 minutes; individual variable.*

Previous skills/knowledge needed

This activity will draw on children's knowledge and awareness of different languages.

Key background information

One of the first Eisteddfodau was held at Cardigan Castle in 1176. Records show that another was held in 1195 at Ystrad Towi. Today, the National Eisteddfod of Wales is held annually in different towns in Wales. There are many performances and competitions such as verse writing, dancing and singing.

Stone circles were built for the ceremony performed by the Gorsedd of the Bards (part of the National Eisteddfod) and can be found all over Wales. Most of the members of the Gorsedd are poets, authors or musicians who have helped to encourage Welsh language and culture. They dress up in blue, green or white robes and welcome new members of the Gorsedd at the stone circle. At other ceremonies two awards of a chair and a crown are made to the best poets.

The Gorsedd of Bards is a relatively new addition to the Eisteddfod. It was initiated by Iolo Morganwg (born Edward Williams in 1747 in a small village in the Vale of Glamorgan). His father was a stone mason and Iolo related that he first

learned his letters from watching his father carve inscriptions on grave stones. He was given books and magazines in English to read by his mother. As he grew up, Iolo became more interested in Welsh poets and authors and Welsh history. Iolo read a tremendous amount and was very knowledgeable. He began to write his own poetry and took the pen name Iolo Morganwg (Ned of Glamorgan). He could even be seen reading books as he walked along some of the roads in Glamorgan.

Iolo was fascinated by the Druids and convinced that the Welsh language was the only Druidic language in the world. Iolo organised the first Gorsedd ceremony on 21st June, 1792 on Primrose Hill in London. A small circle of stones was built and Iolo and his friends swore to defend the Welsh language and culture. Iolo set up Gorsedd meetings in various parts of Wales. In 1819, Iolo persuaded the Eisteddfod organisers at Carmarthen to include a Gorsedd ceremony. It took place in the garden of the Ivy Bush Hotel. Six poets were made members of the 'bardic order' and presented with green, blue and white armbands. Since then, the Gorsedd ceremony has always been part of the Eisteddfod celebrations in Wales. Iolo Morganwg continued to stimulate interest in Welsh history, language and culture until his death in 1826.

Preparation

Prepare the photocopiable sheet on page 156 for each child. Find out if any members of children's families or the local community could come into school to talk about the languages they speak.

Iolo Morganwg

▲ Write the story of Iolo Morganwg. How did he encourage people to know about Welsh language and history?

Resources needed

Photocopiable sheet on page 156 for each child, pencils, crayons and felt-tipped pens. Props which can be used to help tell the story, for example a black top hat, a walking stick, a black coat, a knapsack, a reading book. Examples of words written in different languages.

What to do

Introduction

Talk with the children about different languages. What words do they know from other languages? The quality of this discussion will be dependent on children's own knowledge and linguistic background. Look at some of the examples of words written in different languages and try to say some of them. Explain that many different languages are often spoken in one country.

Development

Tell the children that they are going to learn about how people in Wales have encouraged Welsh to be spoken and written. Talk about the Welsh Eisteddfodau and the Gorsedd of Bards. Use the background information to tell the story of Iolo Morganwg. Ask one child to dress up as Iolo Morganwg, with a black top hat and stick and a knapsack on his back. The child could try reading a book as he walked. Explain how Iolo organised the Gorsedd of the Bards. Do the children think it was a good idea to encourage people's interest in the Welsh language? Ask the children if they think it is a good idea to continue with these ceremonies.

Conclusion

Hand out the photocopiable sheet on page 156 to each child and ask the children to write the story of Iolo Morganwg.

Suggestion(s) for extension

Children might like to organise their own Eisteddfod. They could devise a programme of events. Children could write their own poems and learn dances and songs to perform. The ceremony of the Gorsedd of the Bards could be held. Ask children to sit in a circle and read out poems which they have written. Awards of green, blue and white armbands could be distributed.

Suggestion(s) for support

Some children will need help writing Iolo's story. Ask the children to write three sentences about his life, beginning with his childhood. Alternatively children might choose to draw three pictures illustrating scenes from his life.

Assessment opportunities

Use the photocopiable sheet to help you assess how much information children have acquired about Eisteddfodau and Iolo Morganwg.

Display ideas

Use the activity as a stimulus for creating a display about Wales. Ask the children to collect and bring in objects associated with Wales. These might include: dolls dressed in traditional Welsh costume: objects decorated with dragons; daffodils or leeks; Welsh love spoons; Welsh woollen; examples of Welsh writing.

Reference to photocopiable sheet

The photocopiable sheet on page 156 has a picture of Iolo Morganwg. Children can write about the story of his life and how he encouraged people to be interested in the Welsh language and culture.

King's eldest son) and Sita (Rama's wife) from exile after many adventures and the defeat of the wicked demon, Ravana. To welcome Rama and Sita on their return home, people lit thousands of lights (divas). Diwali also signifies the triumph of good over evil and light over darkness. Sikhs also celebrate at Diwali time and remember the story of the release of the sixth Guru Hargobind Singh from the Moghul Emperor's prison. Hindu and Sikh families celebrate in similar ways: places of worship are decorated and visited; homes are decorated and lit with diva lamps; friends and relatives are visited; cards and presents exchanged; new clothes worn. Parties are held and fireworks set off. At Diwali many Indian women draw 'rangoli' patterns. These are decorative shapes with leaves, flowers and circles which are often drawn outside the door on the ground or on the mud floor of the living room. They are made with rice-flour, spices or coloured chalks. This activity concentrates on ways of celebrating a particular festival; the suggestions for discussion in the introduction of the 'what to do' section could be developed when talking about other festivals and celebrations, for example Hannukah, Holi, Eid, Christmas.

Preparation

Find out if there is anyone in the local community who would be prepared to come into school and talk to the children about Diwali. Prepare table/s in the classroom ready for modelling work. Prepare enough copies of the photocopiable sheet on page 157 for each member of the class.

Resources needed

Plasticine or self-hardening clay (the size of a tennis ball per child). Clay boards or mats, modelling tools, paints suitable for painting the clay. Photocopiable sheet on page 157, crayons, felt-tipped pens. Pictures and books about different festivals and occasions.

DIWALI

To learn about celebrating religious festivals, recognising why such events take place and why they are celebrated in particular ways.

♦♦ *Whole class; individual.*

🕐 *Whole class 20 minutes; individual variable.*

Previous skills/knowledge needed

This activity will draw on children's background knowledge of different festivals and ways in which they are celebrated.

Key background information

Diwali is the Hindu festival of lights which generally falls in November and welcomes in the new year. The story associated with Diwali comes from a famous Indian book, the *Ramayana* and is thousands of years old. Diwali means a 'row of lights'. It commemorates the return of Rama (the

HISTORY KS1

What to do

Introduction

Talk about important occasions which are celebrated and ask the children to describe some of their experiences. Ask the children how they celebrate important occasions: What do you eat?; What do you wear?; What special things do you do? Can the children explain which occasions they celebrate and why? Refer to books and pictures of different celebrations if available.

Development

Tell the children they are going to learn about the festival of Diwali and how it is celebrated. Use the background information to re-tell the story of Rama and Sita. Talk with the children about how the festival is celebrated and explain to the children that they are going to make their own divas and rangoli patterns.

Conclusion

Organise the children into different groups to complete these activities. To make the divas, hollow out a hole from the Plasticine or clay and flatten the bottom. Pinch out a spout and engrave patterns on the outside. When dry, the clay divas can be painted with patterns. Place a nightlight or candle in the diva. Hand out the photocopiable sheet and ask the children to complete it using crayons or felt-tipped pens.

Suggestion(s) for extension

Children may like to design their own rangoli patterns. Diwali can be used as a starting point for children to investigate other festivals of light.

Suggestion(s) for support

Children can complete these activities at their own level according to their different abilities and stages of maturity.

Assessment opportunities

Can the children identify any special occasions and explain how they are celebrated? Do they know any reasons why particular festivals and celebrations are held?

Opportunities for IT

Ramayana Tales from the BBC (BBC Master Computer) enables children to create their own *Ramayana* tale from a library of different pictures.

Children could use an art package to design their own cards to invite their friends to other festivals such as Hanukkah or to celebrate other festivals such as Eid or Christmas. Children could also make a database about different festivals (see 'The Chinese Calendar' on page 101).

Display ideas

Display the divas against a background of silhouetted homes. Ask children to draw their homes on a sheet of black sugar paper about A4 size. Cut out windows and doors and stick yellow paper behind them to give the impression of light shining through. Stick the homes onto a dark background and display the divas at the front.

Celebrate Diwali in the classroom play area. Help children to make paper chains for decorations and make a rangoli pattern on the floor. Diva lamps and Diwali cards can be made. Use playdough to make parathas (savoury pancakes) and balfi (sweets). Provide appropriate clothing for children to wear.

Reference to photocopiable sheet

The photocopiable sheet on page 157 shows a rangoli pattern for the children to complete.

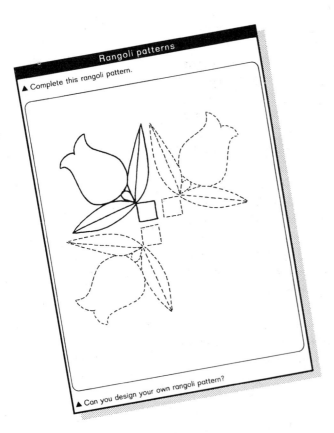

Rangoli patterns

▲ Complete this rangoli pattern.

▲ Can you design your own rangoli pattern?

Photocopiables

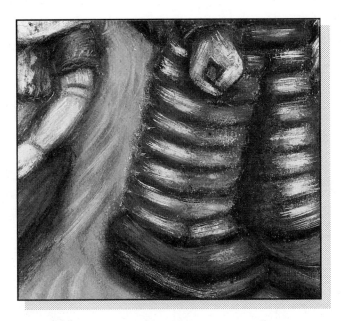

The pages in this section can be photocopied for use in the classroom or school which has purchased this book, and do not need to be declared in any return in respect of any photocopying licence.

They comprise pupil worksheets and resource material for use by the children. There are some pages that have pictures for the children to observe closely and use during an activity. Most of the photocopiable pages are related to individual activities in the book; the name of the activity is indicated at the top of the sheet, together with a page reference indicating where the lesson plan for that activity can be found.

Individual pages are discussed in detail within each lesson plan, accompanied by ideas for adaptation where appropriate – of course, each sheet can be adapted to suit your own needs, and those of your class. Sheets can also be coloured, laminated, mounted on to card, enlarged and so on where appropriate.

Encourage the children to name and date their worksheets and if so required they can be included easily within any pupil assessment portfolio.

Growing up, see page 25

Growing up

▲ Cut out the pictures.
Which objects did you have before you came to school?

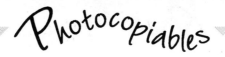

Family generations, see page 27

My generation path

My grandparents' generation

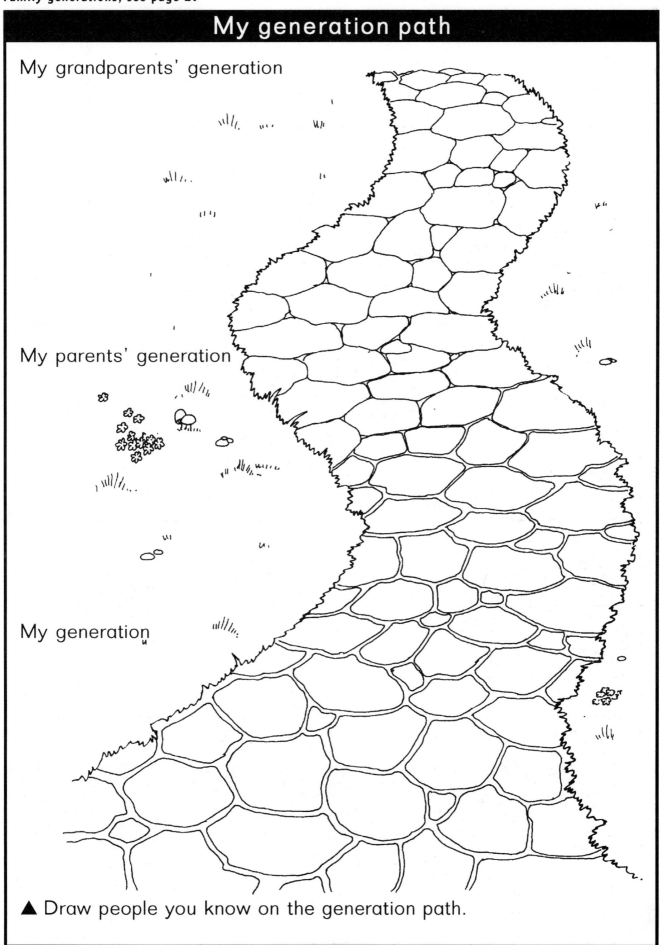

My parents' generation

My generation

▲ Draw people you know on the generation path.

HISTORY KS1

Children's toys, see page 30

Children's nursery – museum display

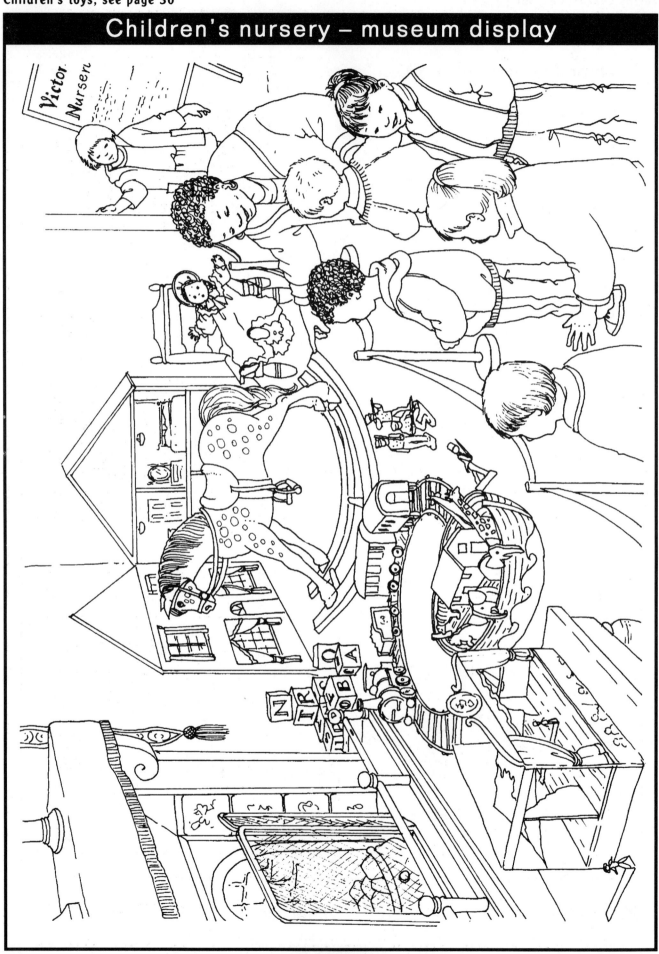

A Homes timeline, see page 32

A timeline of homes

▲ Label the different homes.

a Victorian home

a cave

a Viking home

a detached home

a Tudor farmhouse

_____

_____

_____

_____

_____

▲ Cut out the pictures and put them in order. Begin with the oldest.

Victorian sportswear, see page 36

Victorian sportswear

▲ Draw what you would wear to do these sports today.

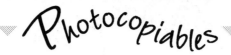

Making woollen cloth, see page 37

Making woollen cloth

▲ Cut out the pictures and place them in order.

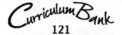
HISTORY KS1

Photocopiables

Learning to write at school, see page 42

Learning to write

Children used sand trays, pencils and slates and pen and ink.

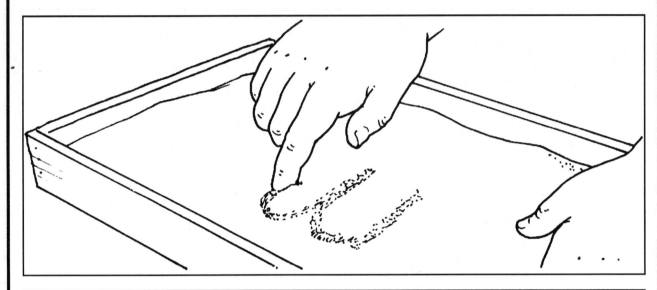

abc

BLACK INK

HISTORY KS1

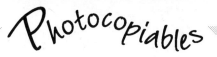
A Victorian washday, see page 44

A Victorian washday

Victorian times	Now

▲ Draw pictures or write about what happens to your washing today.

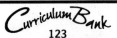

Lighting homes in the past, see page 47

Lighting homes

▲ Draw lines to match the names to the lights.

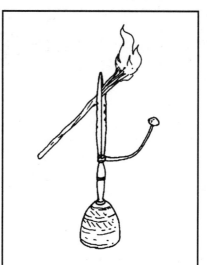

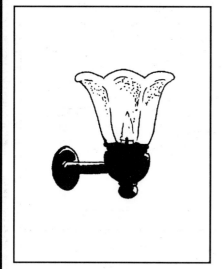

bedside lamp
electric striplight
rush light
Roman lamp
gas lamp
oil lamp
candle
torch

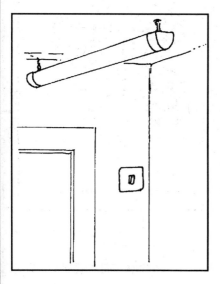

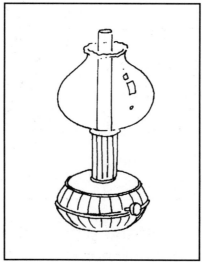

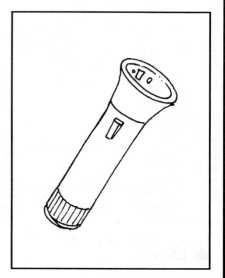

HISTORY KS1

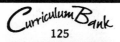

Supplying water to the home, see page 48

Water in the home

▲ Match the labels to the pictures.

_____

_____

_____

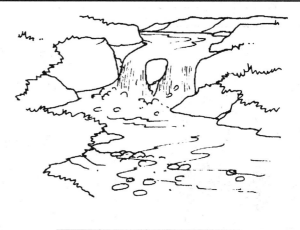

_____

_____

_____

rainwater tub	stand pipe	well
pump	stream	water seller

Inside a Victorian kitchen, see page 50

A Victorian kitchen

A kitchen timeline, see page 52

A kitchen timeline

▲ Cut out the pictures and put them in order. Begin with the oldest.

A ruined castle, see page 55

A ruined castle

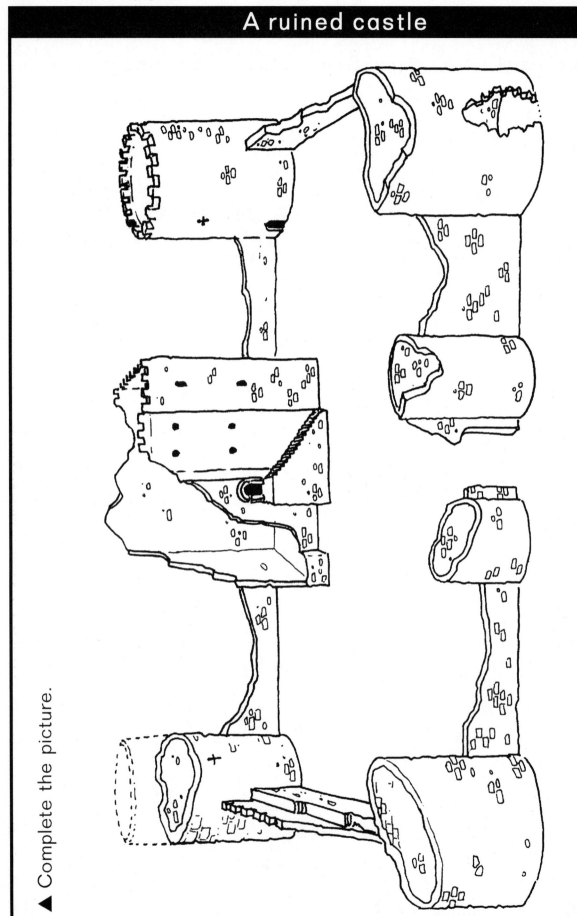

◄ Complete the picture.

◄ Label the **barbican**, **bailey**, **keep** and where the **portcullis**, **drawbridge** and **moat** would be.

Street traders and street cries, see page 56

Street traders

▲ Complete the picture of the street trader.

▲ What goods are being sold?

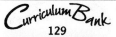

HISTORY KS1

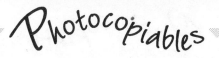

Shop signs, see page 58

Shop signs

▲ Draw pictures to complete the shop signs.

Photocopiables

A Victorian school room, see page 60

A Victorian school room

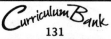

Building different bridges, see page 61

Different bridges

▲ Talk about these different bridges.

▲ What materials are they made from?

Growing corn; the farmer's year, see page 63

Growing corn

▲ Match the old farming pictures with what happens on farms today.
▲ Cut out the pictures and put them in order.

Fire fighting, see page 64

Fire fighting

 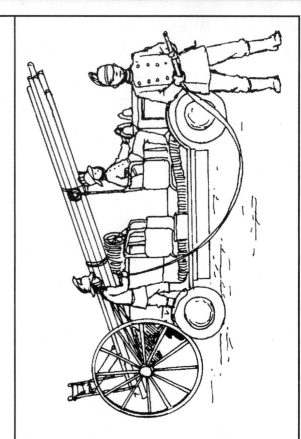

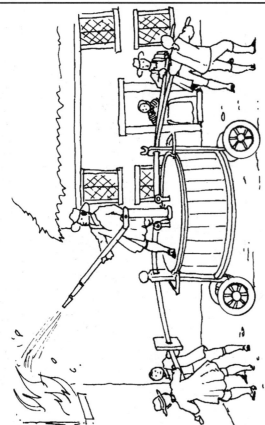 

▲ Cut out the pictures and make a timeline.

Motoring in the past

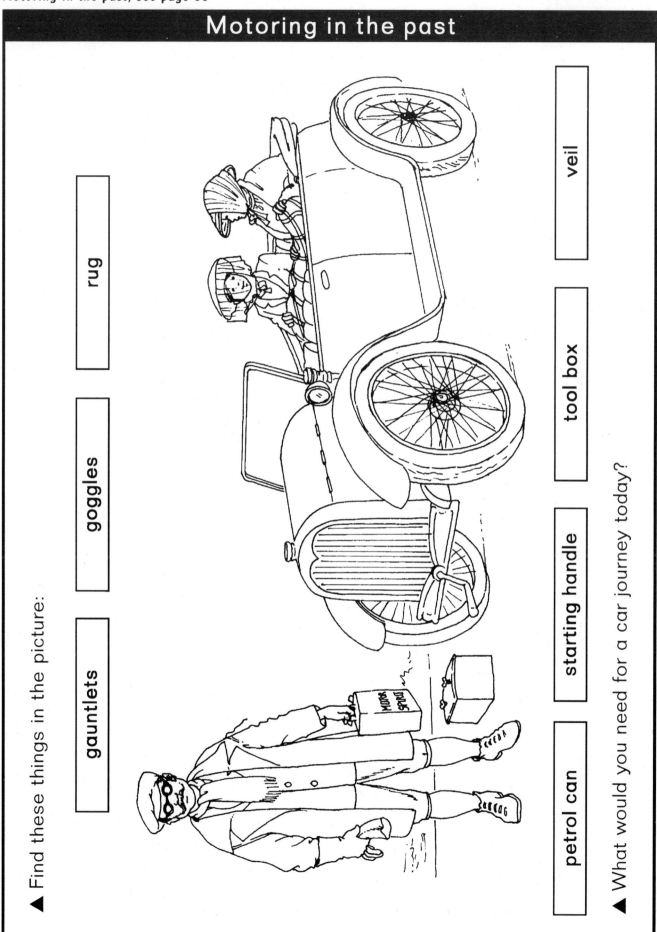

▲ Find these things in the picture:

rug

goggles

gauntlets

veil

tool box

starting handle

petrol can

▲ What would you need for a car journey today?

The bicycle, see page 67

The bicycle

▲ Draw a picture of a bicycle you would see today.

Shipbuilding long ago

▲ What is happening in the pictures?
▲ Complete the last picture to show the finished ship.

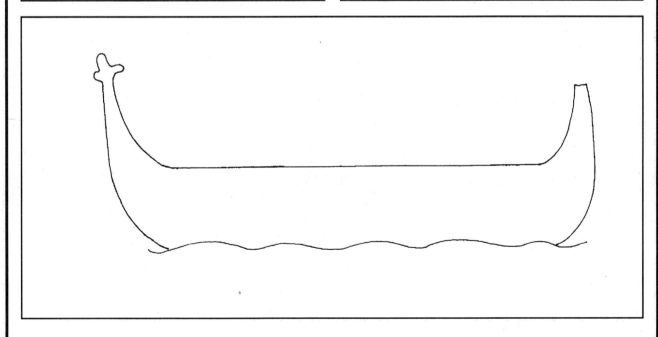

A canal barge, see page 70

A canal barge

▲ Draw someone steering the barge and someone leading the horse.

▲ Complete this sentence:

My barge is carrying ....

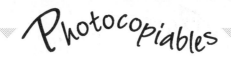

Vehicles in the street 100 years ago, see page 71

In the street

▲ Draw pictures to show what these vehicles would look like today.

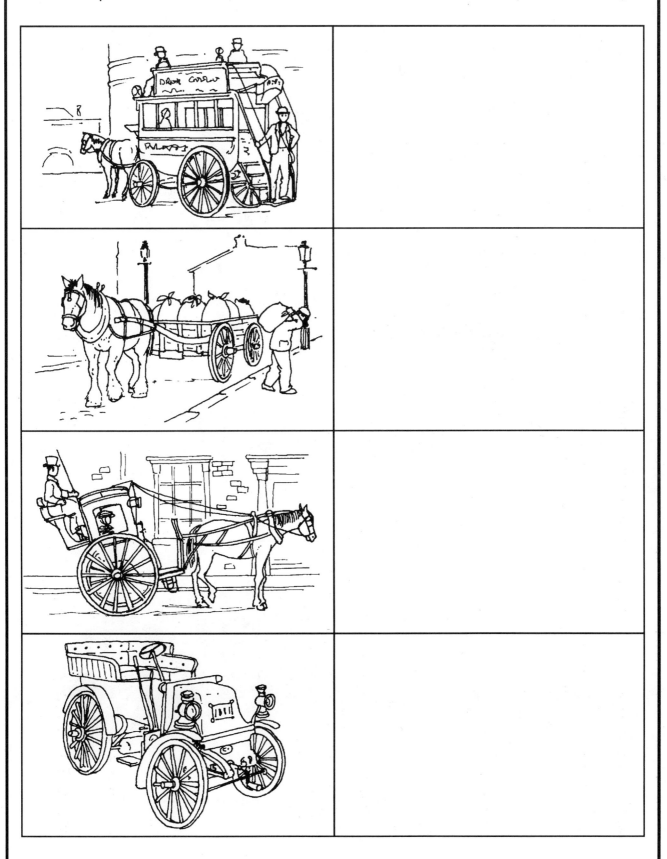

HISTORY KS1

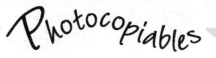

A railway timeline, see page 72

A railway timeline

▲ Cut out the pictures.

▲ Put the pictures in order, beginning with the oldest railway engine.

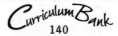

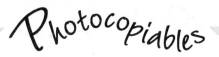

At the seaside

▲ Write about your holiday at the seaside.

HISTORY KS1

Packing a Victorian suitcase, see page 76

Victorian suitcase

Playground games, see page 77

Victorian playground

▲ Can you find children playing these games in the picture?

rolling hoops   hopscotch   spinning tops   leap frog

marbles   tin-can-football   skipping

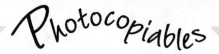

Mary Seacole, see page 83

The wonderful adventures of Mary Seacole

▲ Cut out the pictures and place them in the correct
sequence to tell the story of Mary Seacole.

▲ Draw you own picture in the empty box to add to the story.

Dick Turpin, see page 85

Highway robbery

▲ Complete the Wanted for Highway Robbery Poster.

WANTED

FOR HIGHWAY ROBBERY

_____

_____

REWARD _____

St Hilda, see page 90

Illuminated letter from the Lindisfarne Gospels

John Logie Baird, see page 92

A 1930's television set

▲ Write a slogan to encourage people to buy this television set.

HISTORY KS1

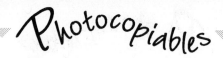
The Terracotta Army

▲ Describe these terracotta soldiers.
What clothes are they wearing? Do they have any weapons?

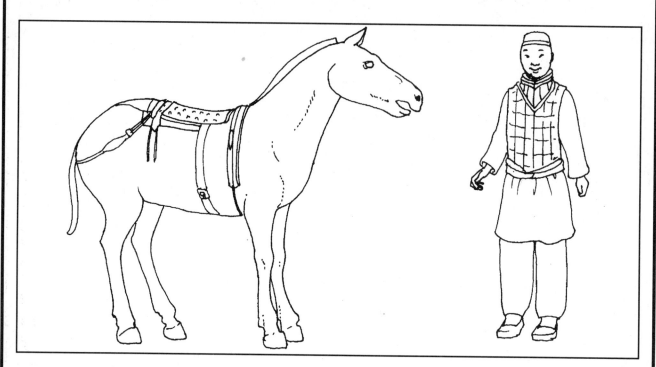

▲ Make a model of a terracotta soldier based on these designs.

Emily Pankhurst, see page 96

Mrs Pankhurst addresses the crowds

▲ Write what Mrs Pankhurst is saying in the speech bubble.

Around the year, see page 100

Changes through the seasons

▲ Draw pictures to show what happens in the different seasons

HISTORY KS1

The Chinese calendar, see page 101

New Year race

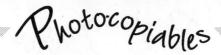

The Battle of Hastings, see page 103

The story of the Battle of Hastings

▲ Connect the sentences to the pictures.
They will tell you the story of the
battle of Hastings.

- **Harold is killed**

- **William sets sail**

- **Harold the King**

- **The ships are loaded with weapons and armour**

- **William leads his men into battle**

▲ Add your own sentence and picture on a separate piece of paper.

The Mayflower, see page 105

Sailing to a new land

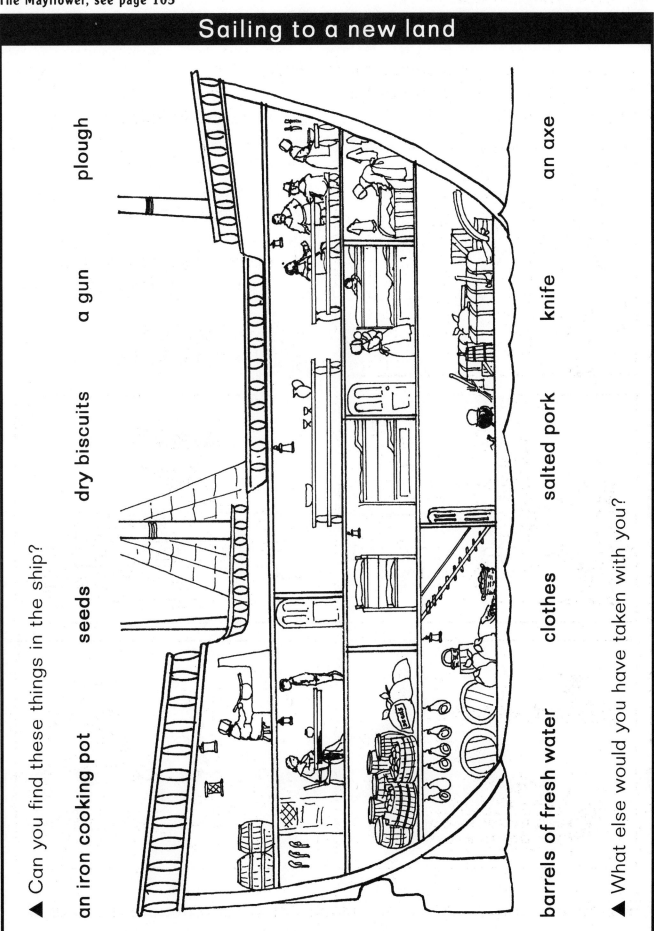

▲ Can you find these things in the ship?

an iron cooking pot   seeds   dry biscuits   a gun   plough

barrels of fresh water   clothes   salted pork   knife   an axe

▲ What else would you have taken with you?

The Great Fire of London, see page 106

The diary of Samuel Pepys

Samuel Pepys wrote about the Great Fire of London in his diary.

September 2nd
I did see the houses at the end of the bridge all on fire....
poor people staying in their houses till the very fire touched them, and then running into boats

September 3rd
About 4 o'clock in the morning, my Lady Bolton sent me a cart to carry away all my money and my plate and best things.....

September 4th
I did dig a pit and put our wine into it
Now begins the practice of blowing up houses ..... it stopped the fire where it was done.

September 5th
I also did see a poor cat in a hole in a chimney, with the hair all burnt off the body and yet alive.....
A sad sight to see how the river looks – no houses, no churches near it.

▲ Record in your diary what you saw of the Great Fire of London.

The Olympic games, see page 110

The Ancient Greek games

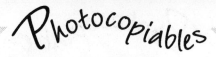

The Eisteddfodd and the Gorsedd of the Bards, see page 111

Iolo Morganwg

▲ Write the story of Iolo Morganwg. How did he encourage people to know about Welsh language and history?

Diwali, see page 113

Rangoli patterns

▲ Complete this rangoli pattern.

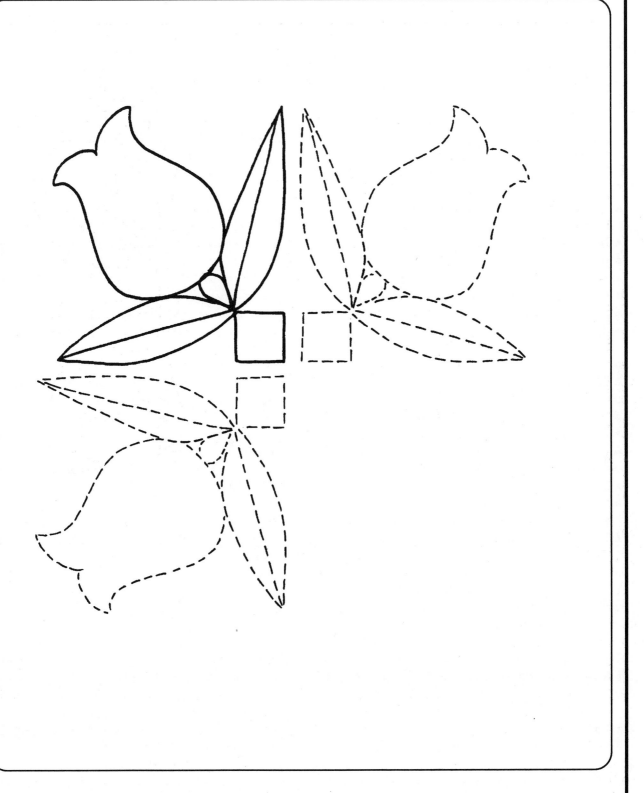

▲ Can you design your own rangoli pattern?

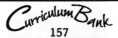

INFORMATION TECHNOLOGY WITHIN HISTORY

The information technology activities outlined in this book can be used to develop and assess children's IT capabilities as outlined in the National Curriculum. Types of software rather than names of specific programs have been mentioned here to enable you to use the ideas regardless of which computer is being used. The main emphasis for the development of IT capabilities within the activities in this book are communicating and handling information.

Word processors

During Key Stage 1 pupils will be developing their confidence and competence to use the standard computer keyboard. They should be taught a range of basic skills including:

▲ an understanding of the layout of the keyboard and where the letter and number keys are found.

▲ how to type capital letters using the shift key.

▲ how to use the delete key to erase words and letters.

▲ how to use the cursor/arrow keys, or mouse to position the cursor at the desired position.

▲ the use of more than a single finger/hand when typing, particularly as they become more proficient and know where letters are located.

▲ how to use the space bar; using their thumbs.

▲ how the word processor will 'wrap' the text around the end of the line (without using the return key).

▲ how to join text using the delete key.

▲ how to separate text using the return key.

▲ how to move the cursor to a mistake and correct it, rather than deleting all the text back to the mistake, making the correction and then retyping the deleted text.

▲ how to print out their completed work (ultimately unaided).

Show the children how to save their work on to floppy disc and how to locate it and retreive it at a later date.

Children can take a long time to enter text at the keyboard so keep the writing tasks short and ideally have an adult (perhaps a parent helper) to hand to advise and assist and if necessary to act as a scribe, keying in the child's ideas

For many of the writing tasks children can use the standard page format that is provided, for more complex tasks you can set up the page layout before the children start and save it, for example, as the menu layout. Children can then start with this basic menu layout and alter it if necessary.

Art packages

A number of simple art or graphics packages are available for children across a wide range of computers. These tend to fall into two categories. The first are graphics packages which enable children to draw lines and shapes and add text. The lines and shapes can be manipulated: resized, moved, stretched and rotated. Colours can be changed and shapes filled. On more sophisticated packages the shapes can be combined together to form a single object, so that, for example, all the components of a house can be drawn separately, combined and then kept as a house. Text can be typed on the page and in some packages different fonts, sizes and colours can be added. In such packages it is easy to move shapes around the screen and position components of a picture wherever you wish. These packages are sometimes referred to as *vector graphics*.

Art or painting packages use a different approach, but can often achieve the same or similar results. The drawing process is more akin to using a pencil or brush. Lines and shapes are drawn by colouring in the individual pixels of the screen. Very detailed work and effects can be produced to create pictures which mirror the results of paint on paper. Such packages usually have a range of tools such as brushes, sprays and rollers for adding and creating different effects. Text can be added, coloured and resized. The scanned images that children make using a hand scanner can be combined in such packages and edited, changing colours or masking out parts of the picture. Such packages are often referred to as *pixel painting packages* and can produce very large datafiles.

The skills that children need to be taught using such software are similar to word processing, but related to pictures. They will need to know how to: select appropriate drawing tools; change features such as line thickness; draw different lines and shapes; edit and erase shapes and lines; resize and rotate shapes and line; move shapes and lines around the screen; select and add colours; add, resize and colour text; save and retrieve their work from a disc; set up the printer and print out their work.

CD-ROMs

There are now a growing number of CD-ROMs available for schools which vary in quality and suitability for younger children. CD-ROMs fall into three broad categories:

▲ The first are those which provide an encyclopaedia type of environment. The CD-ROM will contain text and pictures. Some of the more up-to-date CD-ROMs also include moving pictures and sounds such as music, sound effects and speech.

▲ A second form of CD-ROM is an interactive one, where children make a decision that then takes them to another part of the CD-ROM. These types may be in the form of adventure games or interactive stories. There are also many 'living book' type CD-ROMs which are story books which the children can either read for themselves or hear the words read to them.

▲ The third type of CD-ROM is usually a large collection of pictures or other resources which can be used within the children's own work. There may, for example, be collections of 'clip art' which would be linked to a particular topic such as the Victorians.

The grids here relate the activities in this book to specific areas of IT and to relevant software resources. Activities are referenced by page number rather than by name.

The software listed on the second grid is a selection of programs generally available to primary schools, and is not intended as a recommended list. The software featured should be available from most good educational software retailers.

AREA OF IT	TYPE OF SOFTWARE	ACTIVITIES (page numbers)			
		CHAPTER 1	CHAPTER 2	CHAPTER 3	CHAPTER 4
Communicating Information	Word Processor	24, 25, 27, 29, 30	36, 40, 42, 44, 47, 52, 56, 76	80, 83, 84, 86, 88, 92, 96	100, 105, 106, 108
Communicating Information	Concept keyboard		44		
Communicating Information	Art/graphics	24	39, 58	80, 84, 86	100, 103, 106, 113
Communicating Information	DTP	30	47, 76	83, 86	
Communicating Information	Framework		54		
Information Handling	Database	26, 32, 33	50	92	101
Information Handling	Graphing software	33	45, 48, 71		
Information Handling	CD-ROM		37, 41, 42, 45, 47, 50, 54, 55, 61	81, 83, 94	103, 105, 106, 108
Control	ROAMER/PIPP		72		108

SOFTWARE TYPE	BBC/MASTER	RISCOS	NIMBUS/186	WINDOWS	MACINTOSH
Word Processor	Stylus Folio Prompt/Writer	Phases Pentdown Desk Top Folio	All Write Write On	My Word Kid Works 2 Creative Writer	Kid Works 2 Easy Works Creative Writer
DTP	Front Page Extra	Desk Top Folio 1st Page	Front Page Extra NewSPAper	Creative Writer NewSPAper	Creative Writer
Framework		My World		My World	
Art Package	Picture Builder	1st Paint Kid Pix Splash	Picture Builder	Colour Magic Kid Pix 2	Kid Pix 2
Database	Our Facts Grass Pigeonhole Datashow	DataSweet Find IT	Our Facts Datashow	Sparks Claris Works Information Workshop	Claris Works Easy works
CD-ROM		Children's Micropedia		Encarta Children's Micropedia My First Encyclopedia	
Graphing Software	Datashow	Pictogram Picture Point DataSweet	Datagraph	Datagraph Easy Works	Easy Works

HISTORY KS1

	ENGLISH	MATHS	SCIENCE	GEOGRAPHY	D & T	IT	ART	MUSIC/PE	RE
MYSELF AND MY FAMILY	Making babies' catalogues. Instructions for museum guides. Speaking and listening activities. Sequencing events.	Sorting and grouping different items. Measuring body sizes and weights.	Sorting and grouping different toys.		Designing and making a museum display of children's toys.	Use databases to store and retrieve data on children's heights and weights: birthdays.	Paper weaving balloon baskets.	Singing playground songs and rhymes.	Important occasions in my life. Ourselves and our families.
WAYS OF LIFE IN THE PAST	Writing activities; recording information, making information books, writing instructions; postcards. Role-play and miming activities. Speaking and listening; expressing opinions. Researching further information from different sources.	Measuring the passage of time. Estimating daily water consumption. Measuring and comparing size of penny farthings.	Investigating materials; fabrics, wool, flours, bridges. Sources of power: water mills and windmills, different lighting, ships and boats. Health and hygiene; clean water.	Describing places; sites for wind and water mills, local environment, seaside. Water supply. Shopping. Farming and land use.	Design and make drop spindles, flour mills, time-keeping devices, wells, water pumps, yoke for carrying buckets of water, kitchen spits. Investigate how castles were defended and build own model. Investigate different bike designs.	Program to design coat of arms (eg Paintbox) Data bases to store and retrieve information from kitchen and traffic surveys. Include word processing in discussion on development of writing skills.	Experimenting with different techniques and processes; fabric dyeing, weaving, collage, modelling. Extending experience of different works of art; harvest scenes, Bayeux tapestry, Victorian railway scenes. Individual and group work.	Singing popular songs and rhymes. Devising own street cries. PE: Observing rules for London Bridge is falling down.	Celebrating important occasions. Harvest celebrations.
FAMOUS MEN AND WOMEN	Re-telling stories; written and oral accounts, role-play. Speaking and listening skills; participating in discussion and explaining points of view.	Collect data and organise display of children's favourite TV programmes.	Importance of hygiene for health and safety. Observing and testing objects which float and sink.	Route of Mary Seacole's travels.	Design and test good road surfaces.	Make newspaper report using word processor.	Different techniques and processes; colour mixing, collage, clay modelling. Elizabethan portraits. Illuminated manuscripts and Anglo-Saxon designs.	Singing rhymes; Please to Remember the 5th of November.	People who have helped others. Saints. Discussions on what is 'fair'.
PAST EVENTS AND CELEBRATIONS	Writing activities: Pilgrim Fathers' logs, diaries of Great Fire of London, narrative accounts. Role-play. Speaking/listening/discussion. Research/information retrieval from books.	Symmetrical designs in rangoli patterns.		Effects of seasonal change. Route of Pilgrim Fathers. Locate China on map of the world.	Models of moon landing.		Chinese dragons. The Bayeux tapestry. Collage of Fire of London using silhouettes. Greek art on vases. Modelling divas.	Singing songs and rhymes. Children's own Eisteddfod. Olympic games.	Different celebrations and religious festivals eg Diwali, Chinese New Year. Harvest.